A Dose of Doctrine

Dr. Timothy J. Winters

MOUNT
CARMEL
BOOKS

This book is lovingly dedicated to
my wife, Betty, my partner
in marriage and ministry.

CONTENTS

Foreword

Christianity has been bombarded and confronted with extensive doctrinal lapses. There has been a movement from orthodoxy to sensationalism and emotionalism.

Doctrine has been diluted and distorted to destructive levels, and this has resulted in many heretical and incorrect practices in the Church by the Church, as evidenced by the prevailing obsession and often times ludicrous and innocuous misunderstandings and inept interpretations of Scripture regarding the ministry of the Holy Spirit. This once forgotten person of the Godhead has in recent times received widespread attention and focus by many scholars, denominations and individual believers.

With the revivification of the Pentecostal and Charismatic movement, there has been a deluge of diverse literary and scholarly works dealing with and detailing the ministry and work of the Holy Spirit.

Though the Holy Spirit's presence in the life of the believer is of paramount importance, and though His role must not and should not be underestimated, overlooked or ignored, it is equally erroneous to over-exaggerate and thereby distort the Biblical record concerning the person and work of the Holy Spirit.

In this book, Dr. Winters has concisely examined and brilliantly addressed several key issues and subjects concerning the person and ministry of the Holy Spirit. Dr. Winters shows that there are current beliefs and practices relating to tongues, miracles, gifts of the Spirit, which he discusses are very relevant for all believers and will enable them to have a better and accurate understanding of their relationship with the Holy Spirit.

Dr. Winters also tackles the doctrine of salvation and exposes through good exegetical analysis certain contemporary misguided notions regarding salvation. Dr. Winters brings to the fore relevant Scriptural material that justifies and clarifies a proper understanding of the nature of salvation. The believer will not be disappointed in this succinct but superb study of salvation. Dr. Winters does not side

I

with denomination as he debates the issues surrounding salvation, but he adopts an impartial and effectively balanced perspective that is rooted and grounded in the Scriptures.

Dr. Winters' analysis and study of the Sabbath observance provides us with an insightful and transparent understanding of the meaning and relevance of Sabbath observance for the contemporary believer. Dr. Winters answers the tough questions associated with this issue and through a historical study of the issue he reveals its true meaning and relevance for modern Christianity. This examination by Dr. Winters affords the Christian an opportunity to once and for all understand and clarify the meaning of the Sabbath.

In a culture and time such as this, which is encased in relativism, and clouded with many doctrinal controversies, this book provides all Christians with a sound understanding of right doctrine and right practice. It is necessary for The Church to understand what the Scriptures say about doctrinal issues in order for The Church to eradicate error with right belief. Dr. Winters understands this as he examines several current controversies and gives us Scriptural perspective.

Dr. Winters adeptly addresses these topics without attacking or debasing any denomination or individual. Instead, he focuses on the Word of God as mediator and judge of true doctrine and error, and may we all say with George Goodman:

O Living Word, whose written Word is for our comfort given,
May we heed as if we heard Thy voice that spoke from Heaven.
Let us, as in a mirror, see the glory of our Lord;
And as we gaze, transfigured be His similitude.
From glory unto glory shine, as by the Spirit led,
Into the likeness, all Divine, of Christ, our risen Head.

Dr. E.K. Bailey
Senior Pastor
Concord Missionary Baptist Church
Dallas, Texas

Introduction

Several months ago, I was "pressed in the Spirit" to preach the series of sermons that now comprise this book. The messages were developed in response to the downward drift away from "the apostles doctrine." The trend of un-Biblical teaching is taking deep root in the Church today. I believe we are living in the time that was described by the apostle Paul in 1 Timothy 4:1-3. The warnings of the "Great Apostle" have as much meaning for the Church now as ever before. Sound doctrine is the safeguard for believers in Christ to stay Biblically focused and ultimately remains spiritually healthy.

It is the responsibility of every preacher of the Gospel to warn the people of God to "contend for the faith that was once delivered to the saints." An onslaught of erroneous teachings is spreading in epidemic proportions upon unsuspecting, unprotected, innocent people. Whereupon, it makes the challenge to rightly divide the Word of Truth even more critical. In agonizing pathos the prophet, Isaiah urged his contemporaries to: *"Cry aloud, spare not, lift up your voice like a trumpet, and show my people their transgression."*

Likewise, in our time the challenge for authentic preaching is expressed Scripture.

Holding fast the faithful *word as he hath been taught,* ***that he may be able by sound doctrine*** *both to exhort and to convince the gainsayers. For there are many unruly and vain talkers and deceivers ...****whose mouths must be stopped****.* (Titus 1:8-11)

The title for this book has a medicinal ring to it. A "***dose***" refers to a quantity of medicine. We don't take a dose of food. Therefore, a dose is a measure of something that is taken to improve health. Hence, the health of the Body of Christ requires specific doses of doctrine at various intervals of time.

"***Doctrine***," however, generically means "***teaching***," but the meaning for Christian etymology is the "***core teachings***" of Christ and the apostles. Doctrine is the *"absolute teachings"* of the Christian faith. It is what distinguishes true Christianity from false Christianity. It separates the "saints from the ain'ts." It is the difference between *"authentic Gospel"* and *"another gospel."* To further differentiate genuine doctrine from any other kind of doctrine, the Bible calls it *"sound doctrine."* The word, *"sound"* also has a medicinal ring to it. When we receive good results from a medical exam we are declared to be *"sound."* This is the reason why most wills open with the words, "Being of *'sound'* mind and body, I hereby write my last Will and Testament."

Conversely, since *"sound"* means *"well,"* then *"unsound"* means *"not well."* Since *"sound"* means *"healthy",* then *"unsound"* means *"unhealthy."* The ultimate conclusion then is, as there is *"sound doctrine"* there is also *"unsound doctrine."* Thus, the preaching obligation is not only for *"salvific purposes,"* but for *"sound principles"* as well.

Dr. Timothy J. Winters
Senior Pastor
Bayview Baptist Church
San Diego, California

A Dose of Doctrine

I
The Gift of the Holy Spirit

Now when they heard this, they were pricked in their heart, and said unto Peter and to the rest of the apostles, "Men and brethren, what shall we do?" Then Peter said unto them, "Repent, and be baptized every one of you in the name of Jesus Christ for the remission of sins; and ye shall receive the gift of the Holy Ghost. For the promise is unto you, and to your children, and to all that are afar off, even as many as the Lord our God will call." And with many other words did he testify and exhort, saying, "Save yourselves from this untoward generation." Then they that gladly received his word were baptized: and the same day there were added unto them about three thousand souls. And they continued steadfastly in the apostles' doctrine and fellowship, and in the breaking of bread, and in prayers. (Acts 2:37-42)

1

A Dose of Doctrine

Various inaccurate teachings about the Holy Spirit are circulated today because of a misunderstanding about of the Book of Acts. Urgently, I must say, to use the Book of Acts as the main theology source is, to say the least, risky.

First and foremost, Scriptures must be interpreted in the light of Biblical context and in some cases Biblical context must be supported by **historical context** as well as **cultural context**.

Some time ago, my wife and I spent a week of vacation on the yacht of Dr. Wyatt Tee Walker and his wife, Ann. This is when I discovered that the New York Harbor has three river currents that clash together at one point, making it a treacherous stretch of water. One day, as we headed into the New York Harbor to work our way up the Atlantic Coast, I was at the helm. I had my cap turned backward and my shirt wide open. I was releasing megatons of "*Bayview*" tension with each nautical mile. As we approached a certain point in the harbor, Dr. Walker tapped me on the shoulder and said, "Tim, I better take it now."

I replied, "What's going on man? I'm drivin' this thang'."

He said, "No, you better let me have it now." And he pointed forward of the boat and said, "See right there? Three rivers come together causing dangerous turbulence. An inexperienced helmsman can loose his boat if he doesn't know what's going on."

I yielded the helm and Dr. Walker steered us safely through the harbor.

This illustrates the cautious and skilled maneuvering we have to execute when delving into the Book of Acts. Two contextual currents flow into Acts, they are the **historical context** and the **cultural context**. In the Books of Acts, the historical context is *Jewish history*, and the cultural context is *Jewish culture*. If we are not careful in our maneuvering, we will loose the meaning of its revelation. We must recognize Jewish history and Jewish culture in the background of Acts in order to gain a correct interpretation of its meaning.

The first 10 chapters in Acts are primarily of Jewish emphasis. Peter is the dominant personality in chapters one through 10. However, Paul became the dominant personality from chapter 10 and on to the end of the book. It was the apostle Paul who took the Gospel message beyond the parameters of the Jews to the Gentiles. The separation between Jews and Gentiles was far more drastic than that of African Americans and Europeans in the United States. Jews called Gentiles "dogs."

One occasion that highlights the prejudice of both groups is recorded in John 4:3. This is where Jesus and His disciples had left Judea and were returning to Galilee. When they reached the outskirts of Samaria, Jesus announced to the disciples, *"I must go through Samaria."* That statement both shocked and surprised His disciples, after all, no respectable Jew ever went through Samarian territory. They would cross over the Jordan River and travel north on the other side until they were well past Samaria, and then they would cross back over again to enter Galilee.

Nevertheless, Jesus intended to go into Samaria. Arriving there, He met a woman who had come to the village well to draw water, He asked her for a drink. Her response marked the prejudice from the Samaritan viewpoint. She questioned, *"Don't you know that Jews and Samaritans have no dealings with each other? Why are you asking me for a drink?"*

The Greek word meaning "dealings" carries the meaning of social interaction, particularly, eating and drinking. Fortunately, the story ends better than it began. The woman was ultimately saved, but not until the Lord broke through her entrenched prejudice. Notwithstanding, the Jews' prejudice toward Samaritans and other Gentiles was equally as entrenched. Consequently, the historical and cultural contexts in the Book of Acts must not be ignored. We must be careful as we maneuver through it, or we can certainly miss its meaning.

In Japan there is a fish that is considered a delicacy. However, this highly regarded delicacy is very poisonous except one small section that they consider extremely delectable. However, hundreds of people in Japan die every year from eating this fish. In order to enjoy the eatable portion, the butcher must know exactly what he's doing.

Likewise, when we enter into the Book of Acts for doctrine and theology, we must know what we are doing. It can be a disastrous experience if certain precautions are not adhered to. This is why it is dangerous to "pluck out" one verse and use it as a doctrinal source, particularly Acts 2:38. To lift up Acts 2:38 as exclusive Scriptural authority for salvation is to disregard its Jewish context.

In fact, to lift up any single verse from the Bible as exclusive Scriptural authority is dangerous if you disregard the context. Notwithstanding, most Christians have single source verses that comfort us and give us encouragement. I have a whole bunch that blesses me repeatedly. However, whenever we use only one verse we must be sure that it is in context for fear that it would otherwise produce a meaning that is not consistent with its context.

The purpose of this chapter is to address the Holy Spirit **as a Gift**. This is not to be confused with the **Gifts of the Spirit**. The Holy Spirit bestows gifts for all believers to enable them for ministry, but this is not the Gift of the Spirit nor should it to be confused with the **Fruit** (singular) **of the Spirit**, and certainly not with *"speaking in tongues."*

The Gift of the Spirit is the *person*, the *presence* and the power of the Holy Spirit who is resident in every believer's life. He is the Gift to every Christian or to all believers. The Gift of the Spirit is not available only for a few "privileged" Christians. **Every believer possesses the Holy Spirit**. I call it, "His partnering ministry."

The Holy Spirit partners with us in ministry. He is the reason why we can be bolder than what we usually are. He is the reason that we can be more aggressive and stronger. We all can live better than we live, and we all can do more than we are presently doing because He partners with us.

There is much confusion of *how, when* and *who* can receive the Holy Spirit. Some time ago a young man who was not a member of our Church made an appointment to see me. When he came into my office, he appeared exasperated – confusion written all over his face. He was certainly disturbed about something. I actually thought that he was going to confess some heinous crime, or something worse. He began by telling me that, as a visitor, he was enjoying our Church very much and felt quite comfortable. He related how much he was benefiting from worshipping with us. Then he expressed his quandary. "But, I'm here to ask you why you say 'Hold me up, Holy Ghost' when you're preaching?"

I replied, "Yes, I say that sometimes," wondering what he was getting at.

"But I've always been taught that Baptists don't have the Holy Ghost," he said.

He, obviously, had been exposed to erroneous teaching about the Holy Spirit. From the Scriptures, I explained to him the **indwelling, filling** and several other **functions of the Holy Spirit**. The clear meaning of the Scripture settled his doubts and answered his questions. He is now a part of our Church and is a growing disciple.

Then Peter said unto them, "Repent, and be baptized, every one of you in the name of Jesus Christ for the remission of sins, and ye shall receive the gift of the Holy Ghost." (Acts 2:38)

In some Christian circles, Acts 2:38 is the bedrock verse for salvation. The viewpoint that Acts 2:38 is the nexus for salvation and the Baptism of the Holy Spirit came primarily from the teaching of two men; Thomas Campbell and his son, Alexander, in the latter part of the nineteenth century. Thomas Campbell, a Presbyterian minister, began to interpret Acts 2:38 as the means and authority of salvation. He was convinced that he had discovered the truth in Acts 2:38. His early followers were called "Campbellites."

Today there are entire denominations that base their salvation premise on Acts 2:38. Nonetheless, with regard for the integrity of the Word of God, I vehemently object with the strongest protest I can muster, that to use the Book of Acts as the main theology source for salvation will result in an untrue doctrinal position.

The False Information About the Gift of the Holy Spirit

False information will be contrived from Acts 2:38 if the Jewish history and culture are ignored. The Biblical context for Acts 2:38 starts at verse 14 where the sermon began:

But Peter, standing up with the eleven, lift up his voice and said unto them, "Ye men of Judea and all ye that dwell at Jerusalem, be this known unto you, and hearken to my words." (Acts 2:14)

"Ye men of Israel, hear these words; Jesus of Nazareth, a Man approved of God among you by miracles and wonders and signs, which God did by Him in the midst of you, as ye yourselves also know." (Acts 2:22)

"Men and brethren, let me freely speak unto you of the patriarch David, that he is both dead and buried, and his sepulchre is with us unto this day." (Acts 2:29)

"Therefore let all the house of Israel know assuredly, that God hath made that same Jesus, whom ye have crucified, both Lord and Christ." (Acts 2:36)

From these verses, it is easy to determine the Biblical context of Peter's sermon. Peter was speaking to Jews. The occasion for the sermon was the Day of Pentecost. Pentecost was a Jewish holiday that occurred 50 days after Passover. The few Gentiles that were there were not present among the assembly of Jews where Peter preached this sermon.

For clarification, the Gentiles attendees at this Jewish celebration were called, "Proselytes." A Proselyte was a Gentile who had converted to Judaism.

Note particularly, that the Gentiles (proselytes) *would not have worshipped in the assembly with the Jews*. On the contrary, they would have worshiped in the outer court known as "The Court of the Gentiles."

This means, the message that Peter preached did not fall on Gentile ears.

Furthermore, a highlight of Peter's perception of Gentiles will be enlightening. It was a distorted perception, to say the least. In Acts 10, while on the rooftop awaiting dinner, he had a vision from God. A sheet containing a large quantity of nebulous swarming and slithering creatures was let down before him three times from Heaven. The third time Peter heard a voice:

"Rise, Peter; kill, and eat." But Peter said, "Not so, Lord; for I have never eaten anything that is common or unclean." (Acts 10:13,14)

The purpose of this vision was to prepare him to go preach to a Gentile family. At precisely the time that Peter was objecting to the Lord's command to make his selection for a meal from among the creatures of the sheet, two Gentile messengers knocked at the door inviting him to Cornelius' house to preach the Gospel. Peter reluctantly agreed to go.

In accordance with the Jewish custom of calling Gentiles "dogs," Peter's hesitancy and reluctance were based on his prejudice. It was revealed in his opening comment when he arrived at the house. Instead of the usual cordial greeting of, "Hello, Good morning, Good afternoon or Good evening," Peter made the following statement:

*And he said unto them, "Ye know how that **it is an unlawful thing for a man that is a Jew to keep company, or come unto one of another nation**."* (Acts 10:28)

Lodged deep in the crevasses of Peter's heart was the old Jewish prejudice toward Gentiles. It was only eradicated by the direct divine intervention of God. However, he later confessed, *"But God has shown* (taught) *me that l should not call any man common or unclean."*

Then Peter opened his mouth, and said, "Of a truth I perceive that God is no respecter of persons." (Acts 10:34)

7

God had to work Peter over inside and out before he would preach to Gentiles. **Notwithstanding, when Peter preached** (Acts 2:38), **Gentile salvation was not on his mind.**

Later on (chapter 15) the leadership of Jerusalem Church had to call a special meeting about the matter of salvation for Gentiles. We must understand that the place that Gentiles had in Jewish culture was somewhat like the place we (African-Americans) have had in the American culture for many years, and still have in some cases. We could eat in a public place, but we couldn't eat in a public place with white people. We had to enter restaurants through the rear door and eat in the kitchen. We could drink in a public place – but we couldn't drink from the same public water fountain white people used. We could all use the toilet facilities – but we couldn't use the same toilet white people used. (I really don't think that the toilet made a distinction.)

The interaction of Jews and Gentiles was much like the Jim Crow days for blacks in America. Peter's response to go to Cornelius' house dramatizes the Jewish **historical** and **cultural** context that prevailed during the time of this text.

Consequently, we can see how significant the historical and cultural contexts are in understanding the meaning of Acts 2:38. If we don't recognize it, we'll come away with false information concerning the gift of the Holy Ghost.

For the record, it must be stated that Peter's ministry was primarily to the Jews, and for a time the Jerusalem Church was completely Jewish with a minority of Gentiles who came in later. Today Christianity is *predominately* Gentile in constituency with a *minority* of Hebrews or Jews.

The apostle Paul, who became the dominant person from chapter 13 and on, was called to be an apostle to Gentiles, kings, and the children of Israel (Acts 9:15). Nevertheless, even though he was commissioned to preach to Gentiles, when he arrived in a city, the first place that he would go was the synagogue – *to the Jews first.* He had a message for both the Jews and the Gentiles; that is, until the dispensational door closed on the Jews. In Acts 13:46 he declared:

"It was necessary that the Word of God should first have been spoken to you: but seeing ye put it from you, and judge yourselves unworthy of everlasting life, lo, we turn to the Gentiles."

He stated again in Acts 18:6:

And when they opposed themselves and blasphemed, he shook his raiment, and said unto them, "Your blood be upon your own heads; I am clean: from henceforth I will go unto the Gentiles."

Finally, in Acts 28:28 he announced:

"Be it known therefore, unto you, that the salvation of God is sent unto the Gentiles, and that they will hear it."

From that time the door of opportunity for the Jews was closed. Paul never again tried to reach Jews with the Gospel. The dispensational door had closed.

On the other hand, when Peter preached his sermon on the Day of Pentecost, the invitation of the Gospel was still being offered to the Jews. In fact, it was being offered exclusively to them. This is the historical context behind Acts 2:38 that must be recognized in order to arrive at the true meaning of the text.

Another un-Biblical teaching that is falsely interpreted from the Book of Acts is that people must pray to receive the Holy Ghost. This teaching comes from a "hodge-podge" interpretation of Acts 1:4.

And, being assembled together with them, commanded them that they should not depart from Jerusalem, but wait for the promise of the Father, which saith He, "Ye have heard from me."

The text plainly shows that the Lord certainly did instruct His disciples to wait for the promise. However, historical context is needed to interpret the meaning of His instruction.

The Holy Spirit came on the Day of Pentecost (Acts 2:1). Pentecost comes 50 days after Passover. Jesus died on Passover and remained in the grave for three days and three nights. Furthermore, after His resurrection He continued among His disciples for 40 days (Acts 1:3). That simply means that they had seven days to wait. The Ascension is recorded in Acts 1:9. Following the ascension, they returned to Jerusalem to wait for the Holy Spirit as the Lord had instructed them (Acts 1:12).

The disciples had been instructed to wait for the Holy Spirit, **but the Lord did not instruct them to pray for the Holy Spirit to come**. They prayed, true enough, but not by direction from the Lord. While they waited, their decision to pray was voluntary.

These all continued with one accord in prayer and supplication, with the women, and Mary the mother of Jesus, and with his brethren.
(Acts 1:14)

There was no direction from the Lord in the entire chapter – neither in this verse – for them to pray while they waited. Note that, Mary, the mother of Jesus, was praying with them. They prayed *with Mary*, not *to Mary*.

Nevertheless, the Holy Spirit was coming on the day of Pentecost whether anyone prayed or not. The arrival of the Holy Spirit was not in answer to their prayers. The Holy Spirit was scheduled to arrive on the Day of Pentecost. This verse does not teach that they prayed for the Holy Spirit to come, and it should not be used as authority for requiring Christians to pray for the Holy Spirit.

Philip's revival among the Samaritans found in the eighth chapter of Acts is used for additional support for the teaching that people must pray to receive the Holy Spirit:

But when they believed Philip preaching the things concerning the kingdom of God, and the name of Jesus Christ, they were baptized, both men and women. (Acts 8:12)

*Now when the apostles which were at Jerusalem heard that Samaria had received the word of God, they sent unto them Peter and John: who, when they were come down, **prayed for them, that they might receive the Holy Ghost**: (for as yet He was fallen upon none of them: only they were baptized in the name of the Lord Jesus.)* (Acts 8:14-16)

This is the only case in Scripture where people believed but did not receive the Holy Spirit. Consequently, the apostles were sent there to lay their hands on them. However, this narrative does not produce theology for the Church today that says people are to pray to receive the Holy Spirit, even though that is the clear teaching of some preachers. The Samaritans believed the Word that Philip preached and they were baptized, but did not receive the Holy Spirit. This time the cultural context alone will help to clarify the meaning.

Keep in mind the *strain* that existed between the Jews and Samaritans (and that's putting it lightly). God apparently used their ethnic separation to assure that the apostles would have to interact with the Samaritans. If they had not come to authenticate Philip's ministry, it is likely that they would have remained apart. Let's not forget that the Samaritans already had their own place of worship (John 4:20). Accordingly, the ministry of Peter and John were necessary to heal the split that had been in existence for so many years. Truly, the Church was to be "One Body." Hence, it is not proper to draw from this occasion the conclusion that people must pray and wait for the Holy Spirit, and that an apostle must ultimately lay hands on a person so they can receive the gift of the Spirit. The glaring complexity that this interpretation produces is that *there are no apostles in the Church today* who can perform the necessary function for a person to receive the Holy Spirit.

Another incident that occurred in Ephesus is also used to support the viewpoint that people must pray and wait to receive the Holy Spirit.

And it came to pass that, while Apollos was at Corinth, Paul having passed through the upper coasts, came to Ephesus: and finding certain disciples, he said to them, "Have ye received the Holy Ghost since ye believed?" And they said unto him, "We have not so much as heard whether there be any Holy Ghost." (Acts 19:1-2)

Notice the text does not say, "finding certain Christians." It says that Paul found *"certain disciples."* Paul found certain disciples, not certain Christians or believers. The following verse reveals the identity of these disciples.

And he said to them, "Unto what then were ye baptized?" And they said, "Unto John's baptism." (Acts 19:3)

Then who were these disciples? They were disciples of John the Baptist. You may recall that John the Baptist had a very large following in his day. These people were some of the disciples of John who had heard him say, *"One will come after me who is mightier than I."* As a result, their exposure and understanding had gone no further than what John had taught them. Essentially, they were still under Judaism. They were not Christians. This is why they did not know anything about the Holy Ghost. Paul gave an explanation of why they were ignorant about the Holy Ghost in the next verse.

*Then said Paul, "John verily baptized with the baptism of repentance, saying unto the people, that they should believe on Him who would come after him, that is, on Christ Jesus." When they heard this, they were baptized in the name of the Lord Jesus. And when Paul had laid hands upon them, the Holy Ghost came on them; and they spake **with** tongues, and prophesied.* (Acts 19:4-6)

Superficial observance of this account shows that a group of people (not Christians) had not received the Holy Spirit. They were baptized and Paul laid hands on them. Subsequently, they received the Holy Spirit. Even so, to use this occasion as a theological basis for teaching that Christians must wait to have hands laid on them before they can receive the Holy Spirit is a gross violation of the historical context behind the scene. The main point is that they were not Christians in the first place.

It also mentions *"they spoke with tongues."* They spoke *"with tongues"* and not in *"unknown tongues."*

False information will be extracted from Acts 2:38 if it is not understood that Peter was speaking exclusively to Jews, and that the emphasis of the sermon is on Jesus Christ and not the Holy Spirit. The Holy Spirit is received in consequence of accepting Jesus Christ as Savior. The comparison is like an entree followed by dessert – Jesus being the entrée.

After defending himself the other disciples from accusations that they were drunk, Peter continued on to the main point of his message, Jesus Christ.

"Ye men of Israel, hear these words; Jesus of Nazareth, a Man approved by God among you by miracles and wonders and signs, which God did by Him in the midst of you as you, as ye yourselves also know." (Acts 2:22)

"Men and brethren, let me speak freely unto you of the patriarch David, that he is both dead and buried, and his sepulchre is with us unto this day. Therefore being a prophet, and knowing that God had sworn with an oath to him, that of the fruit of his loins, according to the flesh, He would raise up the Christ to sit on his throne; he seeing this before, spake of the resurrection of the Christ, that His soul was not left in hell, neither His flesh did see corruption. Therefore let all the house of Israel know assuredly, that God hath made that same Jesus, whom ye have crucified, both Lord and Christ." Now when they heard this, they were cut to the heart, and said to Peter and the rest of the apostles, *"Men and brethren, what shall we do?"* Then Peter

said unto them, "Repent, and be baptized every one of you in the name of Jesus Christ for the remission of sins, and ye shall receive the gift of the Holy Ghost." (Acts 2:29-31, 36, and 38)

The primary emphasis of the message is **Jesus Christ**, not the Holy Spirit. Moreover, the requirement of repentance was for **national repentance**, not for **individual repentance**. What national sin had Israel committed? They had crucified Jesus. (In a spiritual sense we are all responsible for the crucifixion of Jesus, but the Jews are also responsible in a literal sense).

*"**Him**, being delivered by the determinate counsel and foreknowledge of God, **ye have taken, and by wicked hands have crucified, and slain**." (Acts 2:23)*

Critical discernment is necessary to see that individual repentance is not a command for salvation. Repentance is not a *condition* of salvation. It is the *consequence* of salvation. Believing in Jesus Christ is the condition. Believing in Jesus Christ produces the repentance for sins. The order is not to first *repent of sins*, but to *recognize the Savior* in order to be saved.

Repentance is in the sequence of salvation, but it is not first in the sequence. Believing Christ and recognizing the Savior is first, and then comes the repentance for sin. You cannot repent of sin until you see the Savior and be saved. In view of this, as lost sinners we were dead in trespasses and in sins. Repentance is not possible when a person is dead. It is the Holy Spirit who brings our dead conscience to life. An illustration of recognizing the Savior first is given in Isaiah.

*In the year that King Uzziah died **I saw also the Lord** sitting upon a throne, high and lifted up, and His train filled the temple. **Then said I, "Woe is me**! for I am undone; because I am a man of unclean lips, and I dwell in the midst of a people of unclean lips: for mine eyes have seen the King, the Lord of hosts." (Isaiah 6:1,5)*

Isaiah most certainly saw the Lord, but he also saw himself. However, the sequence was that he saw the Lord first, and then he saw himself. He didn't say, "*Woe is me,*" until he first saw the Lord. Then he saw his sinful self. It is not sound doctrine to make repentance the perquisite for salvation. When we do, it is like trying to clean fish before we catch them. Another example is when Zacchaeus met Jesus.

And Jesus entered and passed through Jericho. And behold, there was a man named Zacchaeus, which was the chief among the publicans, and he was rich. And he sought to see who Jesus was; and could not for the press, because he was little of stature. And he ran before, and climbed up into a sycamore tree to see Him: for He was to pass that way. And when Jesus came to the place, He looked up, and saw him, and said unto him, "Zacchaeus, make haste, and come down; for today I must abide at thy house." And he made haste, and came down, and received Him joyfully. And when they saw it, they all murmured, saying, That He was gone to be a guest with a man that is a sinner. And Zacchaeus stood and said unto the Lord; "Behold, Lord, the half of my goods I give to the poor; and if I have taken any thing from any man by false accusation, I restore him fourfold." And Jesus said unto him, "This day is salvation come to this house, forsomuch as he also is a son of Abraham. For the Son of Man is come to seek and to save that which was lost." (Luke 19:1-10)

The same sequence is in Luke 19 as it is in Isaiah 6. Zacchaeus made the repenting offer to restore any ill-gotten wealth after he saw Jesus as Savior. Repentance is not required for salvation. It is the result of being saved.

Nonetheless, our repentance is in such close proximity to the point of salvation that it appears to come before salvation. However, in actuality *it comes afterward.* Very few Bible scholars make that distinction. In the same sense, water baptism has the same sequence as repentance. It, too, comes after salvation. However, the teaching of water baptism for salvation is also taken from one verse, specifically the emphasis is to be baptized in Jesus name.

> *Then Peter said unto them, "Repent, and be baptized every one of you, in the name of Jesus Christ."* (Acts 2:38)

False information will always be the result if we don't distinguish between the *literal* and *symbolic* meanings of Scripture. Whenever water baptism appears in Scripture, or is required, it must always be taken symbolically. *Literal cleansing from sin can only be through the blood of Jesus.* Peter certainly said, *"Be baptized everyone of you for the remission of sins,"* but the only meaning that can be deduced from this statement is symbolical.

Since it is *"not possible that the blood of bulls and of goats should take away sins"* (Hebrews. 10:4), then it is also not possible that water can take away sins. In addition to the missed meaning of literal remission of sins and symbolical remission of sins, is the erroneous requirement to be baptized in Jesus' name.

Peter clearly said *"and be baptized in the name of Jesus Christ."* Nevertheless, the command to be baptized in the name of Jesus was to make the name of Jesus *inclusive*, not to make it *exclusive*.

To make the name of Jesus exclusive in a baptismal formula for salvation violates the teaching of the context and the teaching of Matthew 28:19 where the Lord says, *"…baptizing them in the name of the Father, and of the Son, and of the Holy Ghost."*

Peter did not undo or reverse what his Lord had previously taught as the appropriate formula for baptism. In this command Peter was simply highlighting the name of Jesus for *inclusion*. The Jews had *excluded* the name of Jesus. This is seen in the private deliberation of the rulers, elders, and scribes when the apostles were arrested for preaching and performing miracles in the name of Jesus.

> *"What shall we do to these men? For that indeed a notable miracle hath been done them is manifest to all them that dwell in Jerusalem; and we cannot deny it. But that it spread no further among the peo-*

ple, let us straitly threaten them, that they speak henceforth to no man in this name." And they called them, and commanded them not to speak at all nor teach in the name of Jesus." (Acts 4:16-18)

This means that the name of Jesus had been excluded in the Jewish community during the brief time that had elapsed since the crucifixion to the events in Acts 4. Even today, among Orthodox Jews, the name of Jesus is never spoken. The roots of exclusion go all the way back to a time period shortly after the crucifixion. Actually, the authorities essentially told Peter and John that they could preach and teach all they wanted, and anywhere they wanted, as long as they didn't preach in *"that name."*

To them, the name of Jesus is the most reprehensible name among names when, in fact, it is the sweetest name on earth. Here again, the historical and cultural contexts are needed to accurately interpret the meaning of Acts 2:38. This is why the name of Jesus is highlighted and lifted to the forefront by Peter, *not for exclusive use, but for inclusive use.*

Hence, it becomes apparent from the context that Acts 2:38 is not a Scripture for Gentiles. Unfortunately, some Jews *refuse* to use the name of Jesus, and some Christians *confuse* the use of the name of Jesus. Some Christians interpret this verse to mean that you must be baptized in Jesus' name only to be saved and to receive the Holy Spirit. That is false information.

Salvation is not in a *baptism formula* of the name of Jesus Christ, it is in a *bona fide faith* in Jesus Christ.

Inclusiveness was the intention of God in His covenant with Abraham. God said to him, *"In you shall all the nations of the earth be blessed."* The Jews were to be the proponents of the message of the coming Messiah as well as His genetic catalysts, thus giving them the first privilege of the offer of salvation.

"He came unto his own, and his own received him not." (John 1:11)

The early days of the Lord's ministry was exclusively to the Jews.

A Dose of Doctrine

From His own lips the Lord said, in Matthew 15:24: *"I am not sent but unto the lost sheep of the house of Israel."*

However, it must be understood that the offering of salvation first to the Jews was more of *priority* than *exclusion*. The order of priority to the *"Jews first"* carried over into the Apostolic Era.

"For I am not ashamed of the Gospel of Christ: for it is the power of God unto salvation to every one that believeth; to the Jew first, and also to the Greek (Gentile)." (Romans 1:16)

When Peter spoke the words recorded in Acts 2:38, the order of priority was *"to the Jew first"* – strictly Jewish. Some Christian groups, however, have taken Acts 2:38 and made the "Name of Jesus" an essential part of the baptismal formula for salvation. In other words, they teach that people are not saved until a preacher baptizes them in the name of Jesus. The only way to arrive at this interpretation is to ignore the historical and cultural contexts of the Scripture.

You have to ignore the theology from the epistles as well. The baptism in Acts 2:38 is symbolical in the same sense that baptism is symbolic every time that it is mentioned in the Bible.

Similarly, receiving the gift of the Holy Spirit has no literal connection with water baptism. The Holy Spirit does not take up His indwelling presence and minister in us because we have been baptized in Jesus' name. He does not "co-partner" with us because of some formula that a preacher utters when we are dipped under the water. The Holy Spirit is given to indwell us when we believe. This fact is plainly taught by Paul in his letter to the Christians at Ephesus.

That we should be to the praise of His glory, who first trusted in Christ: in whom ye also trusted, after that ye heard the word of truth, the Gospel of your salvation: in whom also after that ye believed, ye were sealed with that Holy Spirit of promise, which is the earnest of our inheritance, until the redemption of the purchased possession, unto

18

The Gift Of The Holy Spirit

the praise of His glory. (Ephesians 1:12-13)

You can see that water baptism is not mentioned in the sequence. We are "sealed" by the Holy Spirit without water baptism. Furthermore, salvation is not possible apart from the indwelling or sealing of the Holy Spirit. He is the "earnest" of our inheritance. Earnest is used in this verse in the same sense of a down payment. The Holy Spirit acts as a security deposit *"until the day of redemption."* The day of redemption must not be confused with the *act of redemption.*

The act of redemption was the death of Jesus on the cross. The day of redemption is when we are resurrected or translated at the rapture. We have the earnest of our inheritance in the presence of the Holy Spirit. He holds and secures us, indicating that someone else wants our souls. After all, there would be no need for Him to secure us if our souls were not in jeopardy of being lost to someone else.

The work of the Holy Spirit is precious to every believer. However, we must be careful in attempting to identify His work in the Book of Acts. Without recognition of the historical and cultural contexts, the interpretation of Acts 2:38 will result in false information.

The Factual Interpretation

The *false information* that is extracted from Acts 2:38 comes out of a *faulty interpretation* and, unfortunately, another unsound teaching that is taken from this verse is that of the Baptism of the Holy Spirit. It is a shame that many Christians are unable to answer correctly and confidently when they are asked, "Have you been baptized by the Holy Ghost?"

Again, "the gift of the Spirit" is incorrectly equated with the "baptism of the Holy Spirit." Even though both occur at the same time, they are distinct works of the Holy Spirit. The "filling of the Spirit" and the "indwelling of the Spirit" occur when the Holy Spirit (the gift) is initially received.

Here I appeal to the golden rule of defining theology in the Bible. The surest place to find theology is to turn to the epistles. The epistles are the theology section of the Bible. It is risky to attempt to find or to define theology from the Book of Acts.

The particular Scripture that defines the baptism of the Holy Spirit is:

For as the body is one, and hath many members, but all the members of that one body, being many, are one body; so also is Christ. For by one Spirit are we all baptized into one body, whether we be Jews or Gentiles, whether bond or free; and have been all made to drink into one Spirit. (1 Corinthians 12:12,13)

The baptism of the Holy Spirit is **when a believer is placed into the "Body of Christ."** In the context of 1 Corinthians 12, Paul likens the Church to a human body, consequently, the phrase "Body of Christ" refers to the Church; that is, the Church as a spiritual entity.

We are not baptized into a local assembly of believers. An individual congregation may appropriately be called "a Church." However, the analogy of a human body does not apply to a local congregation. It applies to the Church, which is sometimes called the "Universal Church," or the "Spiritual Church."

As water baptism means to be placed into water, the Spirit baptism is to be placed into the Church (the spiritual organism.) You may consider it to be a transplant into the Body of Christ.

Just as an organ is transplanted into a *physical* body, a new believer is transplanted into the *spiritual* Body of Christ. When we believe on Jesus Christ as Lord, the sovereignty of the Holy Spirit silently and secretly places us in the Body of Christ. That, my friends, is the baptism of the Holy Spirit.

There is another Scripture that defines the baptism of the Holy Spirit:

"Know ye not, that so many of us as were baptized into Jesus Christ

The Gift Of The Holy Spirit

were baptized into His death." (Romans 6:3)

In this verse, the meaning is to be baptized into Jesus Christ. There is no contradiction. When the interpretation of each verse is coupled together, the meaning is that we are baptized into Christ and into the Church. However, either meaning has spiritual value and makes no sense outside of its spiritual context.

You will have the occasion (if you haven't had it already) to be challenged with the question, "Are you saved?" When you assure the person that you are saved, the follow-up question that will surly be asked is, "Have you been baptized with the Holy Ghost?"

It is shameful that many Christians are stuck on the second question and are vulnerable to an explanation that is based on false information and has been contrived out of the Book of Acts.

It is my desire that every Christian be able to give a Biblical explanation of the baptism of the Holy Spirit. No Christian should be confused or intimidated by questions that inquire, "What did you do when you were baptized by the Holy Spirit?" Or, "What did you feel when you were baptized by the Holy Spirit?"

The correct answer to both of those questions is: "**NOTHING.**"

The baptism of the Holy Spirit is not sensory. You don't feel it. The Neo-Pentecostal movement places heavy emphasis of "experience" and fraudulently attempts to make most of the work of the Holy Spirit something that a person should "feel" or "experience" when, in fact, the opposite is true. We don't feel or experience most of the work of the Holy Spirit.

There are many things that we experience or enjoy that are not sensory; for example, a gorgeous sunrise or a breathtaking sunset. Nevertheless, sunsets and sunrises are not sensory experiences. You can't feel a sunset or a sunrise, but they are real events all the same.

The Bible says that the names of Christians are in *The Lamb's Book of Life*, and they are placed there when we are saved. If I asked you what you felt when your name was put into *The Lamb's Book of Life*, your answer should be, "**NOTHING.**"

The same example holds true for the baptism of the Holy Spirit.

A Dose of Doctrine

If we don't know what the baptism of the Holy Spirit is according to the Bible, untruths can be imposed on us, and we won't know the difference. Do not flinch, hesitate or be intimidated when confronted about the baptism of the Holy Spirit. Be aware that theological teaching cannot be taken from Acts 2:38. Actually, another Scripture has the sequential order:

"In whom ye also trusted, after that ye heard the word of truth, the Gospel of your salvation: in whom also after that ye believed, ye were sealed with that Holy Spirit of promise." (Ephesians 1:13)

The Holy Spirit sealed us after we believed. The baptism of the Holy Spirit is not a separate act from the sealing of the Holy Spirit. The work of the Holy Spirit in salvation is a complete simultaneous work. His work is not a "piecemeal" nor an assembly line operation. Everything that the Holy Spirit does for us is done "after we believe," especially the baptism of the Holy Spirit.

The Faithful Importation

"The Faithful Importation of the Holy Spirit," refers to **receiving the gift of the Spirit**. A superficial reading of Acts 2:38 could be misinterpreted to mean that we receive "the gift of the Holy Spirit" when we have been baptized in Jesus name.

Now when they heard this, they were pricked in their heart, and said unto Peter and to the rest of the apostles, "Men and brethren, what shall we do?" Then Peter said unto them, "Repent, and be baptized every one of you in the name of Jesus Christ for the remission of sins, and ye shall receive the gift of the Holy Ghost." (Acts 2:37-38)

The unfortunate false conclusion comes from not recognizing the historical and cultural contexts of Peter's sermon. The clear teaching from the epistles shows that the Holy Spirit is imported to us when we believe. The context of Peter's sermon does not indicate that receiving the Holy Spirit is based on being baptized in Jesus name. Clearer meaning of the baptism comes in Acts 2:41:

Then they that gladly received his word were baptized; and the same day there were added unto them about three thousand souls.

The baptism was based on his word (the entire word), not just the isolated word that refers to being baptized in Jesus name. The complete context of Peter's sermon was not baptism in Jesus name; neither was it the Gift of the Holy Spirit, it was Jesus Christ. Jesus Christ was the *dominant* and *prominent* theme of the sermon. The sermon covered the Lord's death, burial and resurrection known as the "heart of the Gospel." This was the "word" they received to be saved. No amount of water and no specific words of a baptism formula can result in salvation.

The promise to receive "the gift of the Holy Spirit" was in consequence to believing on Jesus Christ. The shameful and sad fact (actually sinful fact) is that **the Gift** is being prioritized over **the Giver**. This is sacrilege by any measure. It is a basic violation of appreciation and common sense, and is inexcusably ridiculous.

In a general sense, we have the propensity to focus more on our gifts from God than on God who gave them to us. And specifically, there is the tendency to promote the Holy Spirit over Jesus, who gives us the Holy Spirit.

Jesus said, *"And I will ask the Father, and He will give you another Counselor to be with you forever."* (John 14:16)

The Lord told His disciples that He was going away and that the Father would send them the Holy Spirit in His place. Specifically, the Holy Spirit was sent in response to Jesus' prayer. In the same discourse with His disciples, Jesus said:

"But the Comforter, which is the Holy Ghost, whom the Father will send in My name, He shall teach you all things, and bring all things

to your remembrance, whatsoever I have said unto you."
(John 14:26)

Meaning, the Holy Spirit did not come on His own accord. He does not act independently of the Father or the Son. Later on Jesus said, *"And He will testify of Me."*

When Jesus was here, He honored the Father. The Holy Spirit is here now and is honoring the Son. The conclusion is that an improper meaning is being extracted and emphasized from Acts 2:38. The emphasis is on the Gift of the Spirit when in fact Peter's sermon was about Jesus as Messiah.

Thank God for the Holy Ghost, He has work to do that is unique to Himself. Thank God for the Holy Ghost, but Jesus is the source of our salvation. The emphasis should not be on the Gift of the Spirit, but on Jesus who gave the Gift of the Spirit.

II
The Ministry of the Holy Spirit

"And I will pray the Father, and He shall give you another Comforter, that He may abide in you forever; even the Spirit of truth; whom the world cannot receive, because it seeth Him not, neither knoweth Him: but ye know Him, for He dwelleth with you and shall be in you. I will not leave you comfortless: I will come to you." (John 14:16-18)

"But the Comforter, which is the Holy Ghost, whom the Father will send in My name, He shall teach you all things, and bring all things to your remembrance, whatsoever I have said unto you." (John 14:26)

25

I will always remember when my wife and I were on vacation a few years ago. On the first day – not having the usual demands and responsibilities of other days – we laid in bed a little longer that morning. With nothing better to do, I picked up the remote control and began searching for something to watch on TV. Briefly reviewing several channels, I clicked on a very popular television preacher who was preaching a sermon on the Holy Ghost. He ruined my vacation on the first morning.

For the rest of that day and the remainder of that week, I was miserable. Every time it appeared as if I were about to have fun, I would remember what that television preacher said and my spirit would begin to grieve all over again.

What he was preaching has become a popular version of the ministry of the Holy Spirit. There is an unusual preoccupation and promotion of the Holy Spirit in our time. A movement is underfoot that is overemphasizing His ministry – actually, it is being over-exaggerated. It is a renewed emphasis of an old teaching that is called the "Charismatic Movement," once referred to as the "Holy Ghost Movement," and recently known as the "Faith Movement."

It promotes a concept and conclusion that only certain Christians possess the Holy Spirit, along with the viewpoint that acceptance of Jesus Christ as one's Savior is only the initial stage of salvation. The viewpoint holds that receiving Christ and water baptism is only the beginning of the salvation process, and that receiving and being baptized by the Holy Spirit *must* follow.

This teaching attempts to separate accepting Christ for salvation from receiving the Holy Spirit and insists that a person must pray to receive and be baptized by the Holy Spirit. Specifically, a person must pray repeatedly, consistently, earnestly, and urgently until eventually the depth of the prayer touches the Will of God and then He bestows the Holy Spirit unto the awaiting petitioner. This scenario may sound comical to most Christians, but the sad fact is that this is a popular teaching in our time. Additionally, this concept includes the necessity of speaking in so-called "***tongues***" as proof of having received the Holy Spirit.

The Ministry Of The Holy Spirit

But, wait, there's more.

This concept further includes the belief that certain people have the ability enabled by the Holy Spirit to give or pronounce what is known as a "word of wisdom." This is when a person addresses an individual or a congregation with "revelation" directly from the Holy Spirit.

Some time ago, I had two so-called words of wisdom given to me in one day. Neither of the people knew each other, nor were members of our Church. One came in the morning and the other in the afternoon to give me a "word of wisdom" for our congregation. Both "revelations" were ridiculous. I knew their "revelations" were not from God because the work of the Holy Spirit can be examined against the Word of God.

The Holy Spirit Reveals the Savior

If it were possible to prioritize the ministry of the Holy Spirit, revealing the Savior is His foremost responsibility and heads the list of all that the Holy Spirit does.

We all have seen people introduce others who are to speak or preside at some occasion. Some of us undoubtedly have had the opportunity to introduce a speaker, or have been introduced ourselves. How strange would it be if the introducer would introduce himself instead of the person whom he was to introduce? That would be strange indeed. At best, it would be considered odd and improper. If this occurred, the person who was to be introduced would never be known.

In joint session of Congress the "doorkeeper" addresses the Speaker of the House. He says, "Mr. Speaker, the President of the United States," and all of the senators, congressmen and guests rise and applaud the President. At that point the doorkeeper has done his assigned task. However, instead of presenting the President, wouldn't it sound strange for the doorkeeper to present himself instead? Not only would it sound strange, it would be strange.

When General Colin Powell was the chairman of the Joint

A Dose of Doctrine

Chiefs of Staff, he was invited to be the guest speaker at the City Club in San Diego. The president of the club called to let me know that General Powell would be the featured speaker. I had read General Powell's biography and was excited to hear the first African-American chairmen of the joint chiefs speak.

At the luncheon someone was called upon to present General Powell, someone whose name I cannot recall. However, I do remember General Powell, especially his challenge to us to serve with excellence.

But, wouldn't it have been strange if the person who was to introduce the general had introduced himself instead? Wouldn't it have been unusual if the person who was to speak of General Powell had spoken about himself instead? It would have been both strange and unusual. An introducer never presents himself.

Jesus said, "*He* (the Holy Spirit) *shall **testify of Me**.*" (John 15:26)

"*He* (the Holy Spirit) **shall not speak of Himself**." (John 16:13)

Without the introductory ministry of the Holy Spirit, we could not know Christ. He reveals the Savior. The ministry of the Holy Spirit is to Jesus what the ministry of Jesus was to the Father.

Jesus said, "**For I have not spoken of Myself; but the Father which sent Me**, *He gave me Commandment, what I should say, and what I should speak.*" (John 12:49)

In reference to His ministry for the Father, Jesus said, "**I have glorified Thee** *on the earth; I have finished the work which* **Thou gavest Me to do**." (John 17:4)

When Jesus was engaged in His earthly ministry, His work was to introduce the Father. He exalted, promoted and presented the Father. Likewise, the work of the Holy Spirit is to reveal, present and promote Jesus.

28

The Ministry Of The Holy Spirit

"But when the Comforter is come, whom I will sent unto you from the Father, even the spirit of truth, which proceedeth from the Father, He shall testify of Me." (John 15:26)

Notice the words of Jesus: *"The Comforter **whom I will send**..."*

How was the Holy Spirit supposed to get here? Jesus was going to send Him.

When would the Holy Spirit get here? When Jesus sent Him.

This indicates the suborder of the persons of the Godhead. Jesus is subordinate (not inferior) to the Father. Likewise, the Holy Spirit is subordinate (not inferior) to Jesus. You can only send someone whom you have authority over. The end of the verse says, *"He shall **testify of me**."* The Holy Spirit does not testify (speak) of Himself. The primary activity of the Holy Spirit is to reveal the Savior.

*Wherefore I give you to understand, that no man speaking by the Spirit of God calleth Jesus accursed: **and that no man can say that Jesus is Lord, but by the Holy Ghost**.* (1 Corinthians 12:3)

Only by the Spirit can anyone call Jesus "Lord." Our mental capacities cannot comprehend Jesus to be God. Our minds cannot perceive this divine reality. In fact, if we attempt to understand it, *it will "blow" our mind.* The only way a person can recognize and receive Jesus as Lord is through the revealing work of the Holy Ghost. Our understanding of the identity of Jesus is due to the revelation of the Holy Spirit.

An intriguing question that I often ask couples is, "How did you two meet?" Actually, the question isn't as intriguing as the answers often are. I have heard many fascinating stories when couples tell me how they were introduced. However, one thing that's for certain is that your story of how you met your wife or husband won't be the same as my story, but we all have the same story when asked, "Who introduced you to Jesus Christ?" We all have to say, "The Holy Ghost." No one else could have made that introduction.

The teaching that is in wide circulation today hides the person of Christ and highlights the person of the Holy Spirit. Some people make it sound as if the Holy Spirit is speaking more of Himself than of Christ. These innocent people are the product of the preachments that overemphasizes the ministry of the Holy Spirit.

The writing of the apostle Paul reveals deep theological concepts about Jesus Christ:

(Jesus) *who is the image of the invisible God, the firstborn of every creature: for by Him were all things created, that are in Heaven, and that are in earth, visible and invisible, whether they be thrones, or dominions, or principalities, or powers: all things were created by Him, and for Him.* (Colossians 1:15-16)

"...*who is the image of the invisible God*" is a revelation, not a question. Paul was making a statement about the person of Jesus Christ.

*And He is before all things, and in Him all things consist. And He is the head of the body, the Church: who is the beginning, the firstborn from the dead; that in all things **He might have the preeminence**.* (Colossians 1:17-18)

Who deserves preeminence in the Church?
Jesus Christ.
Likewise, who deserves preeminence in our lives?
Jesus Christ.
The Lord's identity is tied to His required preeminence. The point is that Jesus has preeminence, not the Holy Spirit. To listen to some people preach and talk, one would think that the Holy Spirit has the preeminence.

People are being taught to pray to the Holy Spirit. This is popularized in a book titled **Good Morning Holy Spirit.**

The Holy Spirit is not who I speak to when I wake up in the morning. I speak to the Lord first. While on my way to my devotion place, I'm speaking to the Lord and thanking the Lord for the night's rest and for the watch and safety of my family throughout the night. When I arrive at my devotion place, I continue speaking to the Lord.

We are to pray to the Lord. We *are not supposed to pray to the Holy Ghost.* Search the Scriptures and you will see that is what we are to do.

I was once watching a television program that was a forum on marriage. The man being interviewed had become an expert in marriage counseling, and he was asked what keeps his marriage intact. He said that at one time his marriage was not intact. He recognized that it was falling apart. (Praise God for that because some people don't realize that their marriages are falling apart until it is too late. But even more tragic are marriages that are falling apart and the person responsible doesn't realize that he or she is the cause.)

"I returned home from work one day and fell on my knees and prayed to the Holy Ghost to save my marriage," he said.

No, no. Wrong emphasis. Jesus taught us to pray and say, "*Our Father...*" He instructed us to conclude our prayer in His name. We are to pray to the Father in His name, **not in the name of the Holy Ghost**.

I have even noticed that songs are being sung to the Holy Spirit. I heard a song once that went like this:

> *The Holy Ghost saved me,*
> *The Holy Ghost set me free,*
> *I'm just talking about the Holy Ghost,*
> *The Holy Ghost*

That is not what the Bible says. In fact, Jesus says:

> "*For the Son of Man has come to seek and to save that which was lost.*" (Luke 19:10)

Jesus is the Savior. The Holy Spirit is the Keeper. He seals us

A Dose of Doctrine

"until the day of redemption." (Ephesians 1:13) The Holy Spirit seals those whom Jesus saves.

Some time ago, I was in Modesto, California preaching for a friend. He mentioned a new Church that had been constructed, and since preachers like to look at new Church architecture we drove over to see this beautiful "five-star, state-of-the-art" building. I was shocked to see the emblem of the Holy Spirit (the dove) on every door, window, the pulpit, bathrooms and even the door panels to the toilets. This is not proper because Jesus has the preeminence in the Church.

The authentic work of the ministry of the Holy Spirit is to testify of Jesus Christ, not of Himself. The meaning of the Scripture is violated when we place more emphasis on the Holy Ghost than on Jesus Christ. We must always remember that the Holy Spirit reveals the Savior.

He Recalls the Scripture

"But the Comforter, which is the Holy Ghost, whom the Father will send in My name, He shall teach you all things, and bring all things to your remembrance, whatsoever I have said unto you."
(John 14:26)

The Holy Spirit unveils, interprets and instructs from the Scripture. He does not give revelation apart from the Word of God. He will not, and cannot, give revelation apart from the Word of God. When anyone claims to receive a "revelation" from the Holy Spirit and that "revelation" does not connect with the Word of God, allow me to give you a heavy theological term to describe what exactly that is. I'll spell it for you: L- I - E.

In John 14, 15 and 16, Jesus defines the job description of the Holy Spirit. There are restrictive boundaries and perimeters around the ministry of the Holy Spirit. What He does and what He does not do are described in the Scriptures. Even God places restrictions on Himself.

The Ministry Of The Holy Spirit

There are things that God cannot do. For example, He cannot save someone who will not believe. Often times I have heard grieving mourners trying their best to place a dead loved one in Heaven. During the funeral they make all sorts of kind remarks in a eulogy about what a good husband he was, or what a good wife she was. However, when a person has not accepted Jesus Christ, God cannot save them. On the other hand, God will save the vilest sinner who believes on Jesus Christ. God has placed restrictive perimeters on Himself, so there are things He will do and things that He won't do. There are things that God can do and things He cannot do.

When people tell of a "revelation" that they have received from the Holy Spirit, such revelation must have Scriptural likeness. If it lacks Scriptural likeness (I will give you the real theological term this time), it is called an "extra-Biblical experience." People, who give testimonies of experiences that they have had but can't authenticate them with Scripture, have had an "extra-Biblical experience." Meaning, God didn't communicate the "revelation" because it conflicts or confuses written Scripture.

I used to subscribe to a certain magazine in order to keep up with what was going on in the "Holy Ghost Movement," but the "testimonies" in the articles became so bizarre that I stopped reading the magazine altogether. The test of the ministry of the Holy Spirit is the Word of God. However, the testimonies that the people were giving about things that had happened to them violated the Word of God and could not have been of God.

Earlier I mentioned the two so-called "words of wisdom" that I was given by two women on the same day. But if I had known what their intentions were, they would never have gotten an appointment in the first place. Finally, in frustration, when the first women could not convince me that what she was saying was of the Holy Spirit, she blurted out, "You need to let Bayview loose," and followed up by saying that I had the Church too much under control with the Word. To me, this was a compliment. After all, isn't that what a pastor is supposed to do?

Here is Paul's description of a loose Church:

A Dose of Doctrine

How is it then, brethren? when ye come together, every one of you hath a psalm, hath a doctrine, hath a tongue, hath a revelation, hath an interpretation? Let all things be done unto edifying. (1 Corinthians 14:26)

That is what a loose Church looks like. A loose Church is when all the people in the congregation are doing whatever they want to do and blaming it on the Holy Ghost. The Corinthian Church was out of control.

You don't want to be in a Church where there is no order. When God is in control, there is order. By knowing the ministry description of the Holy Spirit, we can maintain our theological balance. Yielding to the ministry of the Holy Spirit is how I maintain a deep level of commitment to Christian service. My strength and endurance are directly related to the responsibility of the Holy Spirit to reveal Scriptures.

There are times when every Christian will feel frustrated, worn down and beaten down. There are times when we all feel like hanging it all up and walking away, never to return. I have had these moments more than I care to admit. If not for the ministry of the Holy Spirit through the Scriptures, I would have succumbed to defeat long ago. At times, through my subconscious, the Holy Spirit recalls Scripture to our memory.

One morning, "the old enemy" poked fun at me about my pastoral leadership. The Holy Spirit did precisely what Jesus said He would do. He placed in my spirit, mind and heart the Word of God. It was a portion of Psalm 46 that reads, *"Be still and know that I am God."*

From that incomplete portion of Scripture, I received the courage and inspiration that I needed. Many nights, while tossing and turning in bed, the Holy Spirit has done what Jesus said that He would do. One night in particular His calming voice whispered to me the words of another Psalm: *"Wait on the Lord and He shall strengthen your heart."*

On numerous other occasions the Word has been, *"Fear not, I am your shield and your exceedingly great reward."*

I was reassured that no matter what is coming up or what is going down, the Lord is my shield and exceedingly great reward.

What about you? Hasn't the Holy Spirit done the same for you? When you were about to say, "That's it. I've had it. I can't take anymore." When you had reached your limit and would have given up, has the Holy Spirit bathed your mind, heart and soul with the memory and meaning of God's Word?

The Holy Spirit not only refreshes us with the promise of God's Word, but also with the power and the provision of His Word. However, it should not be the promise and power that excites us, but God's provision that is His fulfillment of the promise.

"So shall My Word be that goeth forth out of My mouth: It shall not return unto me void, but it shall accomplish that which I please, and it shall prosper in the thing whereto I sent it." (Isaiah 55:11)

This verse serves to assure us of God's provision through His word. It is critically urgent that we search the Scriptures for the revelation and the identification of the ministry of the Holy Spirit. We must diligently search the Scriptures for the delineation of His ministry. He has a *precious, particular* and *perfecting* ministry, as described in the Word of God, but it isn't *popularized* and *promoted* in our times. What is presented as the ministry of the Holy Spirit is a renewed emphasis of an old un-Biblical teaching. Thus, the shortcut to solve all the confusion is to know the Bible because the ultimate test is the Word of God.

It is suggested that the Holy Spirit says things that the Bible indicates that He simply would not say. It is suggested that the Holy Spirit is doing things that the Bible indicates that He would not do. Again, the shortcut is to know what the Word of God says.

The ministry of the Holy Spirit is not a mysterious secret. If you did not know what an apple looked like, someone could tell you that it was an orange and you wouldn't be the wiser. Lack of knowledge leaves us susceptible to ignorance.

A Dose of Doctrine

I am saddened that for some people the Bible is not enough proof to solve this controversy (and other controversies as well). We are in dire trouble when the Bible is not enough proof. Every controversy that arises against the Church today (and we are certainly being tossed, turned and polarized by various controversies) can be answered by the instruction the Lord has given in His Word, settling problems and doubts once and for all.

However, the problem arises when God's Word is not trusted as the ultimate proof when, in reality, it is all the proof that God offers. It saddens me that people hear the plain truth of God's Word but reject it because it does not say what they want to believe. We want it to say "No" when God is saying "Yes." Or, we want it to say "Yes" when He is saying "No." The plain truth of God's Word should settle any controversy if we will only accept its instruction.

The Holy Spirit Regenerates the Sinner(s)

In Ephesians 2:1, Paul describes unsaved people as, "*dead in trespasses and sins.*" While in an "un-regenerated" state, a person is not alert, attentive or attracted to spiritual matters because he or she is dead. Consequently, it is the Holy Spirit who brings to life our spiritually dead conscious through His regenerating work. Paul wrote:

"But the natural man receiveth not the things of the Spirit of God; for they are foolishness unto him; neither can he know them, because they are spiritually discerned. (1 Corinthians 2:14)

The state of being unsaved is death. Everyone knows that you can't communicate with a dead person (well, you can, but it won't do much good). I have seen people during times of grief speak to the dead. I once witnessed a young lady approaching her mother's coffin saying, "Momma, this is me, (she said her name). Momma, answer me, answer me, Momma. Momma. Answer me, Momma."

I silently said to the Lord, "Please Lord, don't let this dead woman answer her, because if you do, Lord, there will be a whole lot more dead people in here."

Needless to say, the dead mother didn't answer her daughter.

Now, I am not making fun of people who talk to their dead loved ones. During the family viewing, I talked to my deceased mother and father, but I wasn't expecting them to answer.

We should ensure that we say all that we intend for our loved ones to hear while they are still living. There's a song:

> *Give me my flowers*
> *While I can smell them,*
> *Speak kind words to me,*
> *While I can hear them*

The Holy Spirit gives life. The old King James Version of the Bible says that He "*quickens*" us. "*Quickens*" refers to making alive. The Holy Spirit regenerates us from death to spiritual consciousness towards God.

When an unbelieving sinner appropriates by faith the work of Jesus Christ on the cross for salvation, at that very moment salvation becomes a personal possession and the Holy Spirit is received instantaneously. The Holy Spirit is not an "after-the-fact" worker in our salvation. He is, actually, at work on our behalf long before our salvation is complete.

The teaching of waiting and praying to receive the Holy Spirit is an unfounded conclusion that is not in the Word of God. It comes from a "hodge-podge" interpretation of when the Lord instructed His disciples to wait for the Spirit (Acts 1:4). The clear order of salvation is as follows:

> *In Whom ye also trusted, after that ye heard the word of truth, the Gospel of your salvation: in Whom also after that ye believed, ye were sealed with that Holy Spirit of promise.* (Ephesians 1:13)

This is the order for the Church today: There is not a command for us to wait and pray for the Holy Spirit.

The sequence is:

In Whom you also trusted...
The Whom is Jesus Christ.
When did we trust in Christ?
...after you heard the Word of truth...
What is the Word of truth?
...the Gospel of your salvation...
...in Whom also, after you believed..."
...you were sealed with the Holy Spirit of promise.

When you believe, you receive and He seals. There is no delay. There is no time lapse between believing on Christ and receiving the Holy Spirit.

Nowadays, an un-Biblical teaching called "slain in the spirit" is being promoted. Perhaps you have seen people laying on the floor of a stage, out cold – or, supposedly, out cold.

A lady once told me about a humorous incident that occurred while she was watching people being "slain in the Spirit." She said a woman fell on stage in front of everyone, but her dress didn't fall properly. So, suddenly her hands moved downward to pull her dress over her thighs. She was supposed to be "slain."

The last time I checked, "slain" meant dead. If she were, in fact, "slain," it wouldn't have mattered that her dress was up over her thighs. How does a dead person's hands move to pull down a dress?

The verse that is used to support being "slain in the Spirit" is found in John 18. Other verses are used for support, but none of them actually refer to "slain in the Spirit." And since this verse is as ridiculous as all the others that are inappropriately used, it will prove the point of idiocy. If you are familiar with this chapter, perhaps you are wondering how someone can be "slain in the Spirit" from its content? The truth is, you can't get "slain in the Spirit" from this portion of Scripture.

We find in John, 18, the story of the arrest of Jesus. The Lord was praying with his disciples (actually the Lord was praying while the disciples were sleeping) in the Garden of Gethsemane. When He had finished His tri-fold prayer, the authorities, led by Judas, came to arrest Him. The Bible says that a "band" of Roman soldiers (the better translation is cohort, 200 to 600 soldiers) came with lanterns, clubs and swords. Jesus asked them, "*Who are you looking for?*" They said, "*Jesus, of Nazareth.*" The Lord replied, "*I am He.*"

Here is the verse:

*As soon, then as He said unto them, "I am (He)," **they went backward, and fell to the ground**.* (John 18:6)

In the statement "*I am, He,*" "***He***" is italicized. This indicates that the word was not in the original manuscript. Jesus didn't say, "*I am, He,*" He said, "***I am.***"

As soon as he said, "***I am,***" the entire cohort of soldiers fell backward on the ground. Remember, these were Roman soldiers. This was an army that had conquered the world. They were dressed in full combat gear, approaching in a fearsome attack formation, *but "as soon, then, as He said unto them, 'I am,' they went backward, and fell to the ground."*

There they were, the fiercest fighting men of that time, on the ground with heels up in the air when Jesus said, "***I am.***"

This is the Scripture that is used to support being, "*slain in the Spirit.*" However, if this is "*slain in the Spirit,*" it is followed by a very peculiar and surprising event.

Then the band (cohort) *and the captain and officers of the Jews took Jesus, and bound Him, and lead him away...* (John 18:12,13)

This means that they got up from the ground and arrested Jesus and took him to His crucifixion. If that is all the good that "slain in the Spirit" produces, then what is all the fuss about? What is so important about being slain in the Spirit? What is the spiritual benefit of it? If all the evil that they had in mind to do to Jesus was still in their minds after they were slain, then what good is it to be *slain in the Spirit*? The truth is, they were not "*slain in the Spirit*." They were knocked down by the released power of His divine presence. This is a blatant misinterpretation and application of Scripture. It is not sound doctrine.

The main purpose for this chapter, however, is to show the work of the Holy Spirit in our salvation. He regenerates the sinner. He brings alive our dead conscience to a new relationship with God.

He Refines the Saints for Service

Christians should not be **showcase saints**. Our purpose after salvation is for service. I have heard do nothing Christians attempt to defend their idleness by saying, "I just try to live mine." This sounds noble on the surface, but the Secret Service is headquartered in Washington D.C. God doesn't need secret servants in His Churches. He needs public servants.

The Holy Spirit refines us for service. This describes His *sanctifying work*. No Christian group has the right to exclusively claim to be sanctified. "Sanctified people" are not a denomination of Christians.

When asked for directions to a *sanctified Church*, most Christians would give directions that would lead away from their own Church. They most likely would say, "Go down to the next intersection and turn north and go three blocks, look on to your left side and you will see a sanctified Church."

That may sound ridiculous, but this happens primarily because of not knowing the meaning of "sanctified." When the Holy Spirit "refines" us, He prepares and sanctifies us for service.

And, there are two areas of sanctification.

Positional Sanctification

Positional Sanctification is when the Holy Spirit sets us apart. We are set apart from the world for the glory of God to be used by

Him. This is the basic meaning of being "sanctified."

The Lord instructed Moses, "*Take off your shoes. The ground that you are standing on is Holy Ground.*" It was sanctified ground. Nevertheless, it was ground like any other ground. It was just as dirty, gritty and grimy as any other ground, but it was Holy Ground. The difference was that God had set it apart.

It is like a sculptor who picks up a lump of clay to fashion it into a specific design. Even though the clay has not been formed or shaped into a design, the sculptor knows what he intends to make, such as a vase, a bowl, or a dish. This equates to *positional sanctification*. In the mind of the sculptor the unformed clay is a vase, a bowl or a dish. However, it won't become anything until the sculptor takes the clay through a process.

Progressive Sanctification

Progressive Sanctification describes the refining (sanctifying) work of the Holy Spirit. It is the progressive process of growth and maturity toward the design that God intends to make of us. The Holy Spirit's ultimate work is to conform us to the image of Christ, which is an ongoing process. *Regeneration* is a work that He does for us at salvation. *Sanctification* is the work He does for us after salvation. A recent song very appropriately describes *progressive sanctification*:

Please be patient with me,
God is not through with me, yet.

An excellent example of progressive sanctification is crude oil that has been pumped from beneath the crust of the earth. It's oil all right, but you can't put it in your Lexus. Why not? It must be refined. It is oil, but it is not ready for service. A new Christian is as saved as any other Christian, but a new Christian is not ready for service. Specifically, the Holy Spirit must refine new Christians to ready them for service unto God.

A Dose of Doctrine

Like sanctification, there is much confusion and misunderstanding about the baptism of the Holy Spirit. The apostle Paul addresses the baptism of the Holy Spirit in 1 Corinthians 12:12:

For as the body is one, and hath many members, but all the members of that one body, being many, are one body, so also is Christ.

Paul used the analogy of a human body to describe the Church, but was not describing a local Church assembly. He describes the Church in its total spiritual entity in 1 Corinthians 12:13:

For by one Spirit are we all baptized into one body, whether we be Jews or Gentiles, whether we be bond or free; and have been all made to drink into one Spirit.

If we can grasp the meaning of ***all*** and ***one***, then we can master the interpretation. All Christians make up the body of Christ and all Christians have the Holy Spirit. However, not only do all Christians have the Holy Spirit, all Christians have been baptized by the Holy Spirit. You can't be a Christian without having the Holy Spirit.

It is funny to hear a person say, "I'm a *born again* Christian." Well, what other kind of Christian can there be except a "*born again* Christian?" We must be *born again* to be a Christian. To be saved we must be *born again.*

So, what is the baptism of the Holy Ghost? It is when a believer is placed into the Body of Christ – the Church – by the Holy Spirit, he or she has experienced the baptism of the Holy Ghost.

...(We) have been all made to drink into one Spirit.
(1 Corinthians 12:13)

Know ye not, that so many of us as were baptized into Jesus Christ were baptized into His death? (Romans 6:3)

42

The Ministry Of The Holy Spirit

When do believers receive the baptism of the Holy Spirit? It's as soon as we acknowledge Jesus as Savior. At that moment, the Holy Spirit sovereignly, silently and secretly places us into the Body of Christ.

What did you feel?

Nothing, with a capital "N."

The baptism of the Holy Spirit is not a feeling. If we didn't know the Word, we would not know that the Holy Spirit had baptized us. It is unfortunate when people try to make the baptism of the Holy Spirit sensory; that is, something that you feel.

The Bible says that when we are saved, our names are placed in *The Lamb's Book of Life*.

What did you feel when your name was placed in *The Lamb's Book of Life*?

NOTHING. It's not sensory either.

The truth is that we would not know what the baptism of the Holy Spirit is, or that our names are in *The Lamb's Book of Life*, if we were not familiar with the Word of God. By no means should we accept any other definition or description of the baptism of the Holy Spirit than what is in the Word of God. The apostle Paul also warns us of being beguiled by enticing words:

> *And this I say, lest any man should beguile you with enticing words.*
> (Colossians 2:4)

Who do you think is involved in beguiling Christians?

Satan.

The first work of Satan was to twist the meaning of the Word of God. That was his first activity, to entice Eve (who in turn enticed Adam) to accept an explanation other than the Word of God. **This Dose of Doctrine** is so that we won't be beguiled:

> *For though I be absent in the flesh, yet am I with you in spirit, joying and beholding your order, and the steadfastness of your faith in Christ. As ye have therefore received Christ Jesus the Lord, so walk ye in Him:*

rooted and built up in Him, and stablished in the faith as ye have been taught, abounding therein with thanksgiving. (Colossians 2:5-7)

This admonition to the Colossian Christians was for them to remain steadfastly rooted in the teaching they had received from the apostle Paul and his associate apostles:

Beware lest any man spoil you through philosophy and vain deceit, after the tradition of men, after the rudiments of the world, and not after Christ. (Colossians 2:8)

If you know what "beware" means then you understand the meaning of this verse. When you see a sign that reads **BEWARE OF DOG**, what do you do? You stand right there at that gate until you can get someone's attention in the house. Words like "beguile" "beware" and "deceit" should get our attention. We are being warned to be aware of anything that is being taught that is not in the Word of God.

For in Him (Jesus) *dwelleth all the fullness of the Godhead bodily; and ye are complete in Him, which is the head of all principality and power.* (Colossians 2: 9-10)

Our salvation is complete in Jesus Christ because of His complete work on the cross.

And you, being dead in your sins and the uncircumcision of your flesh, hath He quickened together with Him, having forgiven you all trespasses; blotting out the handwriting of ordinances that was against us, that was contrary to us, and took it out of the way, nailing it to His cross; and, having spoiled principalities and powers, He made a shew of them openly, triumphing over them in it. (Colossians 2:13-15)

Now, whose word are you going to take?

Whose doctrine are you going to believe?

When people say to you, "Yeah, you're saved but you don't have the fullness." Or, "You're not saved because you need the baptism of the Holy Ghost so that you may speak in tongues."

Whose word are you going to take?

Whose doctrine are you going to accept?

If the Word of God says you are complete, why would you allow anyone to tell you that you are incomplete?

A young man sat in my office one day and complimented me on my preaching. He declared to me that he had been blessed and learned more through our ministry than at any other Church that he had ever attended. Then he said, "But I want more." I asked him, "More what?" He couldn't explain what he meant. He could only express that he wanted more. He felt that there was more of the ministry of the Holy Spirit for him to experience. Later, he left our Church and went where he felt that there was "more."

What more is there above complete?

How much more is beyond complete?

I am grieved when people won't accept the Word of God as their final assurance. As a pastor, the most grievous experience that I have is to set before people the Word of God in plain clarity and have it rejected.

Rejection is much more obvious in a one-to-one setting. After laying out the Word of God the person looks at the Scripture and says, "Hum." He looks at it this way and that way, out of the right corner of his eye, then out of the left corner of his eye, as if that will make it clearer. However, he ultimately refuses to accept the meaning of the Word.

Finally, for every controversy that is in circulation, God's Word has a clear answer.

What word are you going to accept?

Whose word are you going to take?

Right now, at this moment, if you have accepted Jesus Christ as your Savior, you are complete in Him. God's Word plainly states this, and it all begins and ends with the ministry of the Holy Spirit.

III
Tongues, or so-Called Tongues

*For with stammering lips and another tongue will He speak to this
people. To whom he said, "This is the rest wherewith ye may cause the
weary to rest; and this is the refreshing: yet they would not hear."*
(Isaiah 28:11:12)

*And when the day of Pentecost was fully come, they were all with one
accord in one place. And suddenly there came a sound from Heaven as
of a rushing mighty wind, and it filled all the house where they were
sitting. And there appeared unto them cloven tongues like as of fire,
and it sat upon each of them. And they were all filled with the Holy
Ghost, and began to speak with other tongues, as the Spirit gave them
utterance. And there were dwelling at Jerusalem Jews, devout men,*

47

out of every nation under Heaven. Now when this was noised abroad, the multitude came together, and were confounded, because that every man heard them speak in his own language. And they were all amazed and marvelled, saying one to another, "Behold, are not all these which speak Galileans? And how hear we every man in our own tongue, wherein we were born?" (Acts 2:1-8)

"In the law it is written, with men of other tongues and other lips will I speak unto this people; and yet for all that will they not hear me," saith the Lord. (1 Corinthians 14:21)

I feel obligated to state that my motivation for this chapter is not meant to be mean-spirited, nor is it an attack upon those who may teach differently than I do. My purpose is to demonstrate the distressing reality of how misguided emphasis devalues the work of Christ, especially by suggesting that salvation is not complete until a person speaks in "***unknown tongues***."

To suggest that our salvation is incomplete unless we are "anointed" with the gift to speak in "***unknown tongues***" plainly diminishes the work of Christ on the cross and it implies that the Lord's death wasn't enough. My concern is that this notion degrades the work of Christ.

Without reservation, the main controversial activity that is being attributed to the Holy Spirit is the matter of so-called "***tongues***" speaking. I must urgently emphasize that there is a distinction between ***tongues*** and so-called "***tongues***," and it must be recognized that they are not the same. When the reference to "***tongues***" deviates from the Scripture, such reference is not Biblical tongues.

The difference is that one is authentic and the other is not. One is legitimate and the other is not. A twist of irony is that we cannot grasp the difference or perceive the distinction without the help of the Holy Spirit Himself. The Words of our Lord says: "*He will teach us all things and will guide us into all truth.*"

With His illumining guidance into the Word of God, it can be clearly seen that tongues speaking in the Book of Acts and "unknown tongues" speaking in Corinth are not the same. The clarity of the Word shows that what people are "speaking" today is the "***unknown***" version of tongues that took place in Corinth.

A common mistaken liberty is taken when people insert the word "***unknown***" into the Scriptures in the Book of Acts where authentic tongues occur.

And they were all filled with the Holy Spirit and began to speak with other tongues (not in unknown tongues). (Acts 2:4)

The Bible does not say that they spoke with ***unknown tongues***. Consequently, there is no justification for that usage. On the day of Pentecost, they spoke with "***other tongues***" as the Spirit gave them utterance, not ***unknown tongues***. There is a vast difference between "***other tongues***" and "***unknown tongues***."

Intriguingly, the Corinthian Church was the only congregation that had a problem with "***unknown tongues***." No other Church in the New Testament had this problem. We cannot know the truth about the matter of tongues until we see the glaring dissimilarity between "***other tongues***" and ***unknown tongues***. This distinction is critical in order for the truth to be known.

One Sunday between services a deacon showed me a photo collage. It was the veiled image of the face of an old woman. Initially, it appeared as a cluster of various non-descriptive lines. The man held it up and asked, "Pastor, can you see the old woman in this picture?" I said, "Man, I can't see any image at all, animate or inanimate. All I see is a collage of lines."

"Let me help you," he said, pointing to a little dot. "That's her eye."

As soon as he pointed to the small dot the image of her eye became visible. He next pointed to a curved line and said, "That's her chin."

Again, as soon as he pointed to the curved line I could see her chin.

Then he said, "Look at this line. That's the scarf around her head."

After that, he didn't have to point out anything else. I could see the image clearly. It was the profile of an old woman's face. If anyone showed it to me again, I would be able see the image of the old woman immediately.

The topic of tongues is somewhat like that. Once we see it clearly in Scripture, we will see it every time we open the Bible. When we hear the unintelligible "*unknown tongues*," we will know immediately that this was not what occurred in the Book of Acts and that it is not *authentic tongues*.

There are two contextual currents that flow into the Book of Acts, one **historical** and the other **cultural**. Also, as it relates to the entire Bible, we must be aware that there are two main dimensions of time.

There are, of course, eight dispensations, but in simpler terms, only two dimensions of time – one relating to the **Jewish culture** and the other to **Gentile culture**. The two can also be identified as **Old Testament time** and **New Testament time**. When these two time elements are recognized, it will help to solve the controversy about tongues.

It is important to know that there was a time when the Jewish culture was dominant in the Bible. Later, Gentile culture became dominant. The transition of those two times occurred in the Book of Acts.

The dominant Jewish culture did not cease abruptly; nor did the dominant Gentile culture begin suddenly. They overlapped for a short period.

Practically the entire record of the Book of Acts transpired during this short span of time. It is referred to as the *Transitional Period*. There has not been a time like it before or since, simply because the apostles were on the scene. I call them "*God's Bad Boys*," doing what only apostles can do. God used the miracles, wonders and signs of the apostles in a final attempt to reach Israel. Since the Jews were sign seekers, God gave them signs in abundance throughout the ministry of the apostles.

Also, during this **Transitional Period** the Old Testament prophets were still around. Agabus, mentioned in Acts 21, was an Old Testament prophet. He was the one who tied his belt around Paul's wrists and predicted what would happen to him once he arrived in Jerusalem. He was an Old Testament prophet who was still functioning as the Church Age began.

There are no prophets in the Church today who function like the Old Testament prophets. Old Testament prophets *foretold* the Word. New Testament prophets *forth-tell* from the Word.

As mentioned in Acts 21, there also were prophetesses from the Old Testament during this period. Philip's daughters were prophetesses. There are no prophetesses in the Church today. The fact that they appear in the Book of Acts does not mean that their ministry is a New Testament function. It was an Old Testament function that was still operational at the beginning of the Church Age.

To say that this was a very unusual time is an understatement. If we miss the peculiar distinction of that time, we will miss the meaning of "*tongues.*"

The Prophecy About Tongues

The solution to the entire "*tongues*" controversy rests on a prophecy in Isaiah 28:11-12. It is the key that unlocks the door to understanding this confusing issue. If we do not begin here, we most certainly will miss the true meaning of "*unknown tongues*" movement in Churches today.

When I was a boy, my father quit farming and moved the family into town. On occasion a group of us children would get together and go to the movies. It cost nine cents. Once in a while all of us would have a dime at the same time, (which was almost a miracle in itself) and we would go to the movies.

For some reason, we would never arrive at the theater at the beginning of the movie. I didn't even know the show had a start time. All I knew to do was to just go. We didn't call ahead to ask what time the movie started. We couldn't, because we didn't have a phone.

Because we usually arrived at the theater after the movie had already started, we would, initially, never understand certain parts of it. It was only after we watched the beginning that we would completely understand the movie.

This is what is needed to acquire clarity on the subject of tongues. We must start at the beginning, and the beginning is Isaiah 28:11:12:

> *For with stammering lips and another tongue will He* (God) *speak to this people.*

Isaiah was speaking to Israel. God was going to use the language phenomenon of "*stammering lips and* **another** (not unknown) **tongue**" to speak to them.

> *To whom He said, "This is the rest wherewith ye may cause the weary to rest; and this is the refreshing:* **yet they would not hear**.*"*
> (Isaiah 28:12)

The fulfillment of Isaiah's prophecy is in the Book of Acts when Gentiles spoke Hebrew in the hearing of Jews.

> *And they were all filled with the Holy Ghost, and began to speak with other tongues, as the Spirit gave them utterance. And there were dwelling in Jerusalem Jews, devout men, from every nation under Heaven.* (Acts 2:4-5)

The Jews had seven annual Holy Feasts. Three of these feasts required mandatory attendance for all Jewish males 12 years of age and older. The three mandatory feasts were the Feast of Passover, the Feast of Unleavened Bread and the Feast of Pentecost. Consequently, the mandatory requirement for attendance resulted in a teeming numbers of Jews converging into Jerusalem at those three particular times.

> *Now when this was noised abroad, the multitude came together, and were confounded, because that every man heard them speak in his own **language**.* (Acts 2:6)

"*Glossa*" is the Greek word from which we derive our English word, "glossary." In verse 4, it is translated to mean "**tongues**," and is the same word that is translated in verse 6 to mean "**language**." There would be no controversy about tongues speaking if the translators had used the word "*language*" each time. The proponents for "*unknown tongues*" speaking somehow conclude that "*tongues*" is a mysterious unknown language and "*language*" is understandable language. However, this is the meaning of Paul's statement to the Corinthians when he said, "I speak with tongues more than you all." The meaning is that he spoke several languages.

> *And they were all amazed and marvelled, saying to one another, "Behold are not all these which speak Galileans?"* (Acts 2:7)

There was amazement and marveling going on among Jews when this phenomenon occurred. They were surprised that they could understand each other because they had come to Jerusalem "*from every nation under Heaven.*"

The clear meaning is, even though they were all Jews, their versions of the Hebrew language was different from each other. This made it difficult for them to communicate with each other. Even today, Jews who live in Russia speak Russian. Jews who live in Germany speak German. Jews who live in France speak French. Jews who live in the United States speak English.

Though many dialects were represented in Jerusalem at Pentecost, they all understood each other in the language "wherein they were born." *What's more, they understood each other without an interpreter.*

A Dose of Doctrine

"And how hear we every man in our own tongue, wherein we were born?" (Acts 2:8)

It was a surprise that Jews from different countries were able to understand each other. However, take particular note that the language phenomenon at Pentecost happened among Jews. This was before the occasion of tongues speaking by the Gentiles in Acts 10.

Acts 10 records the time when Peter had a vision on the rooftop while waiting for dinner. God let down a sheet from Heaven three times in front of him with the command, *"Rise Peter; kill, and eat."*

On the sheet were all kinds of funny fuzzy looking, crawling creeping things. Peter responded, *"Not so, Lord; for I have never eaten any thing that was common or unclean."*

Not long after, three men who had been sent by a Roman officer named Cornelius arrived. They informed Peter that Cornelius in a vision had seen Peter preaching in his house. They beseeched Peter to return with them, and he went, but with prejudiced apprehensions every step of the way.

When he arrived the first thing he said to Cornelius was, "You know I'm not supposed to be here."

There he stood in the doorway of a man's house with an opportunity to preach the Gospel and all that was on his mind was that it was unlawful for him to be there. This gives us some idea of the prejudicial mindset of Jews toward Gentiles. Nonetheless, he apparently had an instantaneous change of heart because he said: *"God has shown me that I should not call any man common or unclean."*

Then Peter opened his mouth, and said, "Of a truth I perceive that God is not respecter of persons: but in every nation he that feareth Him, and worketh righteousness, is accepted with Him."
(Acts: 10:34,35)

God showed Peter, and ultimately Israel, that divine redemption would go beyond the racial borders of their understanding. *The Jews had the notion that God was their God only.*

Tongues or So-called "Tongues"

In Psalm 48, from which we get the Christian anthem *Let Mt. Zion Rejoice*, the repeatedly emphasized refrain is "*He will be our God*," as if He wasn't God for anyone else.

However, even in the call of Abraham, God indicated that His redemptive plan included all nations. God's call to Abraham included these words:

> "*And in thy seed shall all the nations of the earth be blessed.*"
> (Genesis 22:18)

Peter, of course, did not always understand the broad meaning of God's redemption.

> *While Peter yet spake these words, the Holy Ghost fell on all them which heard the word. And they of the circumcision which believed were astonished, as many as came with Peter,* **because that on the Gentiles also was poured out the gift of the Holy Ghost.**
> (Acts 10:44, 45)

"*Those of the circumcision*" were the Jewish entourage that had come with Peter. They were astonished to see Gentiles being saved.

If the worst sinner in town (if there is such a thing as a worst sinner) walked down the aisle of any Church to accept Christ, no Christian should be astonished. Instead, I hope the people would praise God.

If a "gang-banger" came forward and placed his Uzi upon the altar, why would we be surprised that God would save a gangster?

Nonetheless, Acts 10:45 says that they were surprised because the Gentiles had received the gift of the Holy Spirit with the sign of their salvation being that they heard them speak *with tongues* (language) not "*unknown tongues*" to magnify God." The Gentiles to whom reference is made spoke Hebrew.

> *For they heard them speak with tongues, and magnify God.*
> (Acts 10:46)

55

The next matter for consideration was baptism.

*"Can any man forbid water, that these should not be baptized, which have received the Holy Spirit **as well as we** (Jews)?"* (Acts 10:47)

They had already received the Holy Spirit before Peter mentioned baptizing them. Therefore, when baptism is made essential for receiving the Holy Spirit, it becomes a contradiction to the Word of God. When insisted upon that people cannot receive the Holy Spirit until they have been baptized is a requirement that contradicts what occurred at the home of Cornelius, thus disagreeing with Scripture. This is a classic example of why we should not look to the Book of Acts for theology.

*And the apostles and brethren that were in Judea heard that the Gentiles had also received the Word of God. And when Peter came up to Jerusalem, they that were of the circumcision **contended** with him.* (Acts 11:1,2)

When Peter returned to Jerusalem, the news of his revival at Cornelius' house preceded him, but they didn't applaud him, nor did they roll out the red carpet to receive him. Instead, they **contended** with him, saying:

"Thou wentest in to men uncircumcised, and didst eat with them." (Acts 11:3)

They were upset because Peter had interacted with Gentiles.

But Peter rehearsed the matter from the beginning, and expounded it by order unto them. (Acts 11:4)

Peter's response to their reaction is recorded in verse 4 through 14. He told them about the vision he had while waiting on the roof.

How the men from Cornelius came and invited him to go there to preach.

> *"And as I began to speak, the Holy Ghost fell on them,* **as on us** *(Jews)* **at the beginning.** *Then remembered I the word of the Lord, how that He said, 'John indeed baptized with water, but ye shall be baptized with the Holy Ghost.' Forasmuch then as God gave them (Gentiles) the like gift as he did unto us, who believed on the Lord Jesus Christ; what was I, that I could withstand God?"* **When they heard these things, they held their peace, and glorified God, saying, "Then hath God also to the Gentiles granted repentance unto life.**" (Acts 11:15-18)

This was new theology for a Jewish mind. However, this was only an initial acceptance by the Jewish leaders in the Church at Jerusalem, but it did not transcend into national acceptance by the Jews as a whole. Again, Isaiah 28:11-12 reads:

> *For with stammering lips and another tongue will he speak to this people. To whom He said, "This is the rest wherewith ye may cause the weary to rest; and this is the refreshing: yet they would not hear."*

The ultimate national rejection by Jews that Gentiles could be saved came during the time of Paul's ministry. The first incident happened in Antioch.

> *Then Paul and Barnabas waxed bold, and said, "It was necessary that the word of God should first have been spoken to you: but seeing ye put it from you, and judge yourselves unworthy of everlasting life, lo, we turn to the Gentiles."* (Acts 13:46)

In Acts 18:6; Paul had left Athens to go to Corinth where the same scenario took place there in the synagogue.

> *And when they opposed themselves, and blasphemed, he shook his rai-*

A Dose of Doctrine

ment, and said unto them, "Your blood be upon your own heads; I am clean: from henceforth I will go unto the Gentiles."

The last time that Paul spoke those fatal words to the Jews was when he was in Rome. He began the tirade by saying, *"Well spoke the Holy Spirit by Isaiah, the prophet, unto our fathers."* And he concluded with these words:

"Be it known therefore unto you, that the salvation of God is sent unto the Gentiles, and that they will hear it." (Acts 28:28)

This is a pun from Isaiah 28: *"...they will not hear."* Israel would not hear the Gospel, but the Gentiles would hear it. This is an indication that the door of opportunity was closing on Israel's offer of salvation. Furthermore, it is proved by the fact that in the first century the Church was predominately Jewish but now it is predominately Gentile. Following, Paul gives a clear explanation of the status of Israel:

I say, then, have they stumbled that they should fall? God forbid: but rather through their fall salvation is come unto the Gentiles, for to provoke them to jealousy. (Romans 11:11)

Acts 28:28 not only refers to the fact that Israel rejected Jesus as Messiah, but also their refusal to accept that Gentiles can be saved – even though God had given them the phenomenon of tongue speaking by Gentiles.

Having Gentiles speak in tongues was a sign to Israel. When they heard Gentiles speak in the Hebrew language, they were supposed to know and accept that God would save Gentiles. But as Isaiah s prophecy had predicted, *"...yet they would not hear."*

The Purpose of Tongues

The purpose of tongues is attached to the prophecy of tongues.

58

Tongues or So-called "Tongues"

If the prophecy of tongues had Jewish meaning, the purpose of tongues will have Jewish meaning as well. If the prophecy of tongues concerned Israel, the purpose for tongues also concerned Israel.

What was the purpose?

That divine redemption would go beyond their ethnic interest.

The purpose of tongues was the fulfillment of the prophecy given in Isaiah 28:11-12. Their sign was that they would hear *"...men of other tongues and other lips"* speak to them, yet they did not hear. Consequently, the sign of tongues speaking was for Israel and has nothing to do with Christians.

The Perversion of Tongues

A perversion of tongues was what took place in the Church at Corinth, and what is taking place in Churches today. We are hearing a perversion of tongues. It is a perversion regardless of how sincere the person may be that is "speaking" in *"unknown tongues."* The person may love the Lord sincerely, but the sounds are nothing more than incoherent noise – a perversion of the real thing.

Tongues in the Book of Acts were authentic. What occurred in the Church at Corinth was counterfeit. What occurred in the Corinthian Church is noted by the word *"unknown."* There were no *"unknown tongues"* spoken in the Book of Acts.

The Apostle Paul admonishes us to *"follow after love."* The proponents of speaking in *"unknown tongues"* as the Corinthians did, have made *"unknown tongues"* an improper priority.

Follow after charity, and desire spiritual gifts, but rather that ye may prophesy. (1 Corinthians 14:1)

These inspired words were written by Paul to rearrange the improper priority that the Corinthians placed on *"unknown tongues."* The correct emphasis was to prioritize love.

Though I speak with the tongues of men and of angels, and have not

A Dose of Doctrine

charity, I am become as sounding brass or a tinkling cymbal. (1
Corinthians 13:1)

Paul admonished them that love was the priority over all spiritual gifts. The instruction is that nothing is wrong with desiring
spiritual gifts. However, if we desire a spiritual gift, we should desire
to prophesy so that there may be edification. Prophecy and edification are the priorities that should head the lists of the spiritual gifts:

*But he that prophesieth speaketh unto men to edification, and exhor-
tation and comfort. He that speaketh in an unknown tongue edifieth
himself; but he that prophesieth edifieth the Church.*
(1 Corinthians 14:3-4)

*How is it then, brethren? when ye come together, every one of you
hath a psalm, hath a doctrine, hath a tongue, hath a revelation, hath
an interpretation. Let all things be done unto edifying.*
(1 Corinthians 14:26)

Once again, the priority is prophecy and edification. The Greek
word meaning prophecy is *"profteia,"* which means to foretell or
speak under inspiration. The New Testament version for prophecy
is to **forth-tell** the Word. The Old Testament version for prophecy
was to **foretell**.

Many misinformed people are attempting to bring the Old
Testament style of prophecy into the Church today. Preachers and
pastors are prophets in the sense of **forth-telling** the Word.

The attempt to prophesy in the Old Testament sense is done
through an exercise known as giving "a word of wisdom." In this
chapter we will see the *revelation*, the reason and the *requirement* for
the priority of prophecy and edifying.

*For he that speaketh in an unknown tongue speaketh not unto men,
but unto God: for no man understandeth him; howbeit in the spirit
he speaketh mysteries.* (1 Corinthians 14:2)

Tongues or So-called "Tongues"

A big part of the confusion and misunderstanding concerning speaking in "*unknown tongues*" comes from misinterpretation of this verse. In the King James Version of the Bible, the word "*unknown*" is italicized.

When a word is italicized in the Bible, it means that it was not in the original manuscript. The translators added certain words for a smoother flow from the Hebrew or Greek languages in an effort to communicate a clearer meaning of the passage. Sometimes a passage is clearer with the added word, but sometimes not.

In this case "*unknown*" does not make the passage clearer. However, the intent for placing "*unknown*" in the text was *to indicate that what was being spoken by the Corinthians, was not a language*. It was an "*unknown language*."

The addition of "*unknown*" in the text was to indicate that it was *incomprehensible* speech. **The only time "*unknown*" is italicized in all of the New Testament is in this chapter**.

The word "*unknown*" only appears three times in the entire New Testament. In each case the meaning is clear. However, "unknown" is only italicized in 1 Corinthians 14:2 to indicate unintelligible speech.

*For he that speaks in an unknown tongue **speaks not unto men, but unto God***.

This verse is erroneously used to declare that when people speak in "*unknown tongues*" they are speaking to God and not to men.

Let us not forget that spiritual gifts are not for God, they are for the Church, the Body, so we can be edified. **God is not edified by our spiritual gifts.** If I preach alone at home to God, who would be edified? God doesn't need the Gospel. As a pastor, my gifts are for the Church (the Body of Christ). Other people's gifts in the Church are for me.

Furthermore, the Greek word behind "God" in the aforementioned verse is "theos." It is an interesting word because it can be translated to mean the real *God*, or a false *god* or *gods*. The context in which it is used determines if "*theos*" should mean God or false god(s). **In this case it means false gods**.

This is when, as well as why, historical context and cultural context are so critical in interpreting the Scripture.

The historical and cultural context for the Corinthian people is that they had come out of a pagan religious background that included using esthetic utterances to speak to false gods. This is the meaning of verse 2. They were not speaking to God, but rather to their former pagan gods. They had slipped back into their former style of using esthetic utterances to communicate to their "god."

Additionally, their conduct at the Lord's Supper was a throwback to their pagan practice of gorging themselves and getting drunk at their pagan "Love Feast." They also engaged in temple prostitution that had been brought into their Christian worship from their previous pagan practices.

When a man was "burdened," he could go to the priestess and have his "burdens" rolled away. Or, if a sister was "burdened" she could go to the priest and have her burden "rolled away."

Or, even if a man wanted another man or a woman wanted another woman, he or she could go to Church (as they used to do in their temple) and get their "burdens rolled away." This explains their lack of concern of the man who was "sleeping" with his father's wife.

And, of course, they had brought into their Christian worship the old pagan custom of "ecstatic utterance," which is unintelligible speech sounds. It would help us to know that the Buddhist chants are esthetic utterances. They are not in the Chinese or any other oriental language. The same is true of the Hare Krishna chants, which are esthetic utterances as well.

*...for no man understands him; however **in the spirit he speaks mysteries***. (1 Corinthians 14:2)

We have to do the same thing with the word "*spirit*" that we did with the word "*God*" to get the true meaning. The translators attempted to provide us with the meaning by *not* capitalizing "*spirit.*"

The Greek word for spirit is "*pnuma.*" It can mean the Holy Spirit, human spirit, or evil spirit. To determine which "spirit" is meant, we must pay attention to the context in which it is placed, which will dictate the proper meaning.

Here, the context shows Paul's meaning was not that "in the Holy Spirit a person speaks mysteries." God does not speak in mysteries. The "mysteries" were the unintelligible sounds that they were making. The word, "spirit" is used in this verse in the same sense that it is used in verse 14. The meaning is human spirit. The *human spirit* was producing mysterious sounds.

For if I pray in an unknown tongue, my spirit prayeth, but my understanding is unfruitful. (1 Corinthians 14:14)

"*My spirit*" means the human spirit. This does not mean praying by inspiration of the Holy Spirit. Jesus has given instructions about how the Holy Spirit would speak.

"*Howbeit when He, the Spirit of truth, is come, He will guide you unto all truth: for He shall not speak of Himself; but whatsoever He shall hear, that shall He speak: and He will shew you things to come.*" (John 16:13)

The Lord said that the Holy Spirit would speak what He tells Him to speak. The Lord never spoke in mysteries. Multitudes of people did not follow Him because He spoke mysteries. The Bible says that the common people heard him gladly.

The Scriptures record the occasion when His enemies returned from their surveillance and told the authorities, "*Never have we heard a man who speaks like this Man.*" They didn't make that confession because He was speaking in mysteries.

Another time, His enemies said, "*He does not speak as the scribes. We understand Him.*"

Mysterious speaking was not a teaching technique of Jesus, and neither was it characteristic of God in Old Testament times. God told the prophet Habakkuk to *"Write the vision and make it plain."*

So, Paul rebuked the Corinthians for speaking in mysteries. In fact, God has always clashed with mediums, witches, wizards and people who use witchcraft and satanic séances and mysterious communications. God used His prophets to confront them. Mysterious speech is not of God. God speaks plainly.

Again, I call attention to the preference of prophesying for edification.

He that speaketh in an unknown tongue edifieth himself, but he that prophesieth edifieth the Church. (1 Corinthians 14:4)

What could be plainer?

The first point of clarification is that "**unknown tongues**" are not spoken to God, but to gods.

The second point of clarification is that **the person who speaks in "*unknown tongues*" edifies himself, or herself**. Again, the preference is prophesying because it edifies the Church.

The admonishment for the previous verses is followed by an acknowledgement.

I would (desire) *that ye all spake **with tongues** (not **unknown tongues**), but rather that you prophesied: for greater is he that prophesieth than he that speaketh with tongues, except he interpret, that the Church may receive edifying.* (1 Corinthians 14:5)

This is a reference to real "**tongues**" (languages). However, even then there must be an interpreter so that the Church can receive edification. The significance is that even a real language cannot give edification if there is no interpretation. Nowhere in this chapter has Paul given an admonishment or command for an interpreter for "**unknown tongues**." There is no interpretation for an "**unknown tongue**," which is meaningless.

Tongues or So-called "Tongues"

Now, brethren, if I come unto you speaking with tongues (real tongues), what shall I profit you, except I shall speak to you either by revelation, or by knowledge, or by prophesying, or by doctrine. (1 Corinthians 14:6)

Paul makes a strong case for the worthlessness of even real tongues that are spoken without a specific purpose or meaning. In other words, for "real language" communication, there must be an objective for the vocalizations.

And even things without life giving sound, whether pipe or harp, except they give a distinction in the sounds, how shall it be known what is piped or harped? For if the trumpet give an uncertain sound, who shall prepare himself to the battle? So likewise for you, except ye utter by the tongue words easy to be understood, how shall it be known what is spoken? for ye shall speak into the air. (1 Corinthians 14:7-9)

Even inanimate life produces sounds that we can recognize, such as the roaring waves of the ocean (I love that sound). Anytime I hear the sound of ocean waves I know the meaning of that sound. Nothing else resembles it. The sound of the ocean is distinct, but every ocean worldwide sounds the same.

Things without life (inanimate) produce sounds, such as a flute or a harp. And, what's more, they produce a distinct sound. A flute does not sound like a harp, nor does a harp sound like a guitar. They all have their own distinct sound.

This gives meaning to the question that comes in verse 8.

If a trumpet makes an uncertain sound, how shall we prepare for battle?

I can blow a bugle (or, at least, make some sounds). But, hopefully, the Lord would be merciful on the army that had me as a bugler. When I blew the bugle they wouldn't know whether it was reveille, retreat, or time to go to bed, because all I would be doing would be making "***uncertain sounds.***"

There are, it may be, so many kinds of voices in the world, and none of them is without signification. Therefore if I know not the meaning of the voice, I shall be unto him that speaketh a barbarian, and he that speaketh shall be a barbarian unto me.
(1 Corinthians 14:10-11)

Of all the "many kinds of voices in the world," none are without signification. All languages provide intelligible verbal communication. The use of the word "barbarian" does not have the meaning we affix to it today. A barbarian was anyone who did not speak Greek.

The analogy can extend to fowls and animal life. All birds have their own distinct sound. A bird does not sound like a lion and a lion does not sound like a horse. They all produce their own distinct sound. In the case of fowls and animals, the distinction of sound provides the meaning of the sound. The meaning is the species that can be identified by the sounds.

Wherefore let him that speaketh in an unknown tongue pray that he may interpret. (1 Corinthians 14:13)

The context of this verse show that "***unknown***" should not have been added here. The admonishment is to pray to interpret. This is the clue because there is no interpretation for an "***unknown tongue.***"

This verse deals with an actual case of legitimate language, and even then the interpretation is the priority. The idea is that a person who speaks in a tongue should want to interpret, or to have the communication interpreted. In ether case, the priority gift is interpretation so the Church may receive edification, as stated in 1 Corinthians 14:5.

Tongues or So-called "Tongues"

For if I pray in an unknown tongue, my spirit prayeth, but my understanding is unfruitful. (1 Corinthians 14:14)

First and foremost, it must be understood that Paul is using a hypothetical scenario to address the practice of praying in tongues. In no way should this Scripture be used to support *"praying"* in tongues. The hypothetical nature of the verse is obvious from the words "...**if I pray in an unknown tongue...**"

However, the meaning of the statement is not hypothetical but instructional. When people pray in a *"tongue"* their spirit is the motivation, not the Holy Spirit. And, what's more, they don't even understand what they are saying.

This comment by Paul lets us know that the congregation at Corinth was also *"praying in **unknown tongues**."* And, not only did they pray in *"**unknown tongues**"* (according to verse 15), they were also singing in *"**unknown tongues**."*

They were speaking in *"**unknown tongues**," praying* in *"**unknown tongues**," singing* in *"**unknown tongues**,"* gorging themselves and getting drunk at the Lord's Supper, and engaging in all kinds of sexual immoralities. *"**Tongues**"* was a major part of their worship and, obviously, just a part of their inability to comprehend Christ's teachings.

With only a shallow cursory overview of the Scriptures, it will reveal that no place in the Old Testament or the New Testament is there any instruction to the saints of God to pray in tongues.

People who allegedly *pray* in *"**unknown tongues**,"* use the following verse to incorrectly justify their actions:

Likewise the Spirit also helpeth our infirmities: for we know not what we should pray for as we ought (should): But the Spirit itself maketh intercession for us with groanings which cannot be uttered.
(Romans 8:26)

It is certainly possible to be burdened or frustrated to the extent that we are unable to pray. It has happened to me more than a few times. However, during those times the Word of God assures us that "the Spirit Himself makes intercession for us with groaning that cannot be uttered."

This Scripture is *unfortunately*, and *incorrectly*, interpreted to be a "prayer language" for the saints.

How can this be a prayer language?

This is the ministry of the Holy Spirit in His indwelling capacity. It is the intercession ministry of the Holy Spirit for us.

However, this verse is used, along with 1 Corinthians 14:14, as the Biblical authority to pray in tongues. The advocates of "*praying in unknown tongues*" interpret the "groaning" to be the person who is praying in "*unknown tongues*." It is thought to be a special, mysterious "prayer language."

But, the Scripture plainly says, "*The Holy Spirit Himself makes intercession for us with groaning.*"

It is the Holy Spirit who speaks to God for us in groaning. When Jesus arrived at the tomb of Lazarus, He "groaned" in His spirit.

Whatever the communication between the Holy Spirit and the Father, Paul describes it as "groaning." It is a communication between the Persons in the Godhead.

We don't make the groaning, nor do we hear the groaning. Our knowledge of this peculiar communication by the Holy Spirit comes through the revelation of the Word of God. All that we know and are able to know is that the Holy Spirit makes intercession for us with groaning. We are not praying (especially in "*unknown tongues*"). The Holy Spirit is praying for us.

The classic instructions to Christians on praying are given by Jesus Himself.

"*But thou, when thou prayest, enter into thy closet, and when thou hast shut thy door, pray to thy Father which is in secret; and thy Father which seeth in secret shall reward thee openly. But when ye pray, use not vain repetitions, as the heathen* (pagans) *do: for they think that they shall be heard for their much speaking.*" (Matthew 6:6-7)

Tongues or So-called "Tongues"

The clear command to Christians from the Lord is that we should not pray like pagans (don't forget the pagan background of the Corinthians). Specifically, the instructions indicate that we are not to use "vain repetitions" like the pagans do when they pray.

The Greek word for "vain repetitions" is "*battalogeo.*" "*Batta*" means to stammer or stutter. "*Logeo*" means word or words. "*Battalogeo*" is to repeat the same words or sounds over and over.

If you ever have heard a record "stick," then you will understand the meaning. Some of us remember how the needle would sometimes stick on an old 45 record and the same lyric would be repeated over and over. We are not to do that when we pray. That is "vain repetition."

An English word that helps the meaning of the Lord's instructions on prayer is "*onomatopoeia.*" It is *intelligible* sounds repeated over and over. Children, "playing cars" make "onomatopoeia" sounds of a car.

In contrast, "*battalogeo*" is *unintelligible* sounds repeated over and over.

Ecstatic utterances (the imitation noise called "**unknown tongues**") are "*battalogeo*" sounds. But, even repeated *intelligible* sounds do not communicate and are annoying.

When the record stuck we would quickly bump the needle arm so it could continue, because hearing the same lyric over and over is not pleasant. The same is certainly true of repeated *unintelligible* sounds. If repeated *intelligible* sounds are annoying, then repeated *unintelligible* sounds are even more annoying.

So-called "**tongues**" are nothing more than *unintelligible* sounds repeated over and over that don't mean anything.

Some time ago, I watched a young lady on television introducing a solo that she was about to sing. She talked in English a while, but then would mumble an esthetic utterance. She went back and forth between English and esthetic utterance. But what she mumbled was the same sound each time.

If you listen to people who are supposed to be speaking in "**unknown tongues**" you will hear the same sound each time. It is

69

never longer or shorter. It is the same sound.

Any Greek theology text or Greek dictionary will define "batta-logeo" to mean, *"meaningless, mechanical, repeated phrases"* and will reference pagan modes of prayer mentioned in Matthew 6:7.

The perversion of tongues that was going on in the Corinthian Church is the same perversion that is permeating Churches today.

The Place of Tongues

The place of tongues is expressed in 1 Corinthians 14:22.

*Wherefore **tongues are for a sign**, not to them that believe, but to them that believe not: but prophesying serveth not for them that believe not, but for them which believe.*

Paul quotes Isaiah 28:11-12 in the previous verse to prove that the Corinthians had the wrong interpretation and understanding of tongues. Verse 21 states:

In the law it is written (referring to Isaiah), *"With men of other tongues and other lips will I speak unto this people; and yet for all that will they not hear me," saith the Lord.*

The Jews had refused their sign. And, *"**tongues**"* are a sign. The word, "believe," as it is used in this Scripture, does not identify a believer (a saved person). It identifies the Jews who did not believe that Gentiles could be saved, so God gave them a sign.

The ironic feature about the matter of *"**unknown tongues**"* is that the advocates for *"**tongues**"* have made this to be a Christian sign. However, the truth is, there is no longer a place in the Church for this sign because God no longer needs it for Israel. People are unknowingly making a sign intended for the Jews a Christian sign. It is called the "evidence" of salvation.

If you have ever missed a sign while driving, then you are famil-iar with the inconvenience of having to drive miles out of your way to get back to where you are going. This is the case with "***unknown tongues.***" It is an extreme inconvenience to attempt to make "***unknown tongues***" a Christian practice. It is not our sign.

When I drive to Los Angeles from San Diego there are various signs for many coastal cities along the way. But, those are not my signs. My sign is Los Angeles.

At the city limits there is a sign that reads "Welcome to Los Angeles." However, no motorist ever stops at that sign. We drive on past the sign into the city of Los Angeles.

Signs merely point to the real thing. That's why no one crawls up on a billboard and tries to drink from the image of a Coca-Cola bottle. It is just a sign. "***Tongues***" was a sign to Israel that Gentiles would be saved. Since God (for the time being) has set Israel aside, there is no place for that sign in the Church.

As stated at the opening of this chapter, it detracts from the complete work of Christ on the cross to insist that people are not saved until they speak in "***unknown tongues.***" It diminishes the perfect work of Christ on the cross.

I am simply attempting to speak the truth in love. This book is not (and certainly not this chapter) personally directed to any one individual, nor is it directed to any Christian group that believes "***tongues***" speaking is essential for salvation.

However, it is unfortunate that in light of the clear teaching of Scripture that some people believe that their salvation is incomplete until they speak in "***unknown tongues.***"

From the cross Jesus said, "*It is finished.*" "Finished" means complete. The Lord has never done incomplete work. Everything that God does is complete.

God's army has never left the battlefield saying, "Whew! We barely won that one."

When God wins a battle, it is complete.

Our salvation is complete in the fact that we were once dead in trespasses and sins, but Christ has made us alive.

And ye are complete in Him. (Colossians 2:10)

For this reason, it is ridiculous to say that people do not have salvation until someone lays hands on them and prays so that they may "get" the Holy Ghost and speak in "***unknown tongues***."

Who is responsible for our salvation?

Is it Jesus or the person who prays and lays hands on people?

Our salvation is complete in Jesus Christ. In the words of the old hymn, "*Jesus paid it all.*" And, I'd like to add that He also paid the principal and the interest.

There is no issue that has divided, or is dividing, the Church like the matter of so-called "***tongues***." However, the apostle Paul gives a simple conclusion to the problem.

> *For God is not the author of confusion, but of peace, as in all Churches of the saints.* (1 Corinthians 14:33)

The simple conclusion is that God is not the author of confusion, but of peace. When there is confusion you can be sure that God did not cause it. It means that someone was not clearly listening to Him.

We must keep in mind what the first activity of Satan was to undermine the Word of God. The temptation in the Garden was an attack on the authority, the integrity and the fidelity of the Word of God – and that is still the evil one's target today.

The apostle Paul dealt with the same confusion and controversy regarding so-called "tongues" as we are seeing today in our Churches. However, with all that Paul writes to correct the error of "tongues," some people use the following Scripture in an attempt to show that he supported speaking in "unknown tongues."

> *Wherefore, brethren, covet to prophesy, and forbid not to speak with tongues.* (1 Corinthians 14:39)

The advocates for speaking in "***unknown tongues***" emphasize this verse because Paul admonishes the Corinthian congregation to "...*forbid not to speak with tongues.*"

Tongues or So-called "Tongues"

With each stroke of his inspired pen, Paul condemns and forbids so-called "*tongues*." This statement, however, applies to the times when real "*tongues*" (languages) were being spoken among the Corinthians, and is not to be confused with "*unknown tongues*."

If any man speak in an unknown tongue, let it be by two, or at the most by three, and that by course; and let one interpret.
(1 Corinthians 14:27)

Actually, the word "*unknown*" should not have been inserted in this verse because he says, "*...let one interpret.*" There is no interpretation for an "*unknown tongue*." Real tongues were still operative – to a degree – at the time Paul wrote this. Even then, he says, "*...let it be by two, or at the most three, and that by course; and let one interpret.*" The instructions were "*...and that by course*" meant one person was to speak at a time.

Every time my family gets together, someone has to stand up several times and tell all of us to "be quiet." Because we often haven't been together in a long time, we are very excited and talk over each other – everyone speaking at the same time. It is utter chaos and no one can understand what anyone else is saying. This is what happens when people talk at the same time.

My wife once watched a pastor on the television who instructed his entire congregation to stand up. He then said, "One, two, three, go." And they took off in ecstatic utterances. There was no interpreter.

Even if "*tongues*" were a function of Christians today, such speaking would have to be done according to the Bible. Show me a Church that practices speaking in "*unknown tongues*" with no more than three people speaking in sequence.

Some time ago when on a preaching assignment in New York City, I learned that the Barnum and Bailey Circus was also in town and performing at Madison Square Garden. I had never been to a circus, or Madison Square Garden. This was my chance to "kill two birds with one stone," as my father would say – take advantage of two opportunities in one.

So we paid our money and went inside. It was just as advertised, a "three-ring circus." However, it was the most disappointing entertainment we ever paid for in our lives. We didn't know which ring to look at because there was too much going on at the same time. We didn't know whether to watch the guy eating fire, or another guy who had an elephant sitting down on a small three-legged stool. In the other ring there was a lion jumping through hoops of fire. We simply didn't know what to watch. We left in bewilderment before the show even ended.

I later learned that circus entertainment is primarily designed for children, and now understand why children enjoy circuses so much. It is because a child doesn't pay attention to details.

Paul said not to be like children because, as adults, we must pay attention to details. There are specific detailed instructions in the Word about speaking in "*unknown tongues*." And, when those instructions are ignored, the result will be as chaotic as a circus.

I once heard a story about a young boy who observed some men setting up a tent, which thought was for a circus in his community. He was excited because he had never been to a circus and wanted desperately to see one. Later that evening he was disappointed when he discovered that instead of a circus, it was a tent revival.

When the boy grew up, he had a longing for God in his heart. So he went to Church looking for a revival, but instead saw a circus.

But if there be no interpreter, let him keep silence in the Church; and let him speak to himself; and to God. (1 Corinthians 14:28)

This does not mean to speak to God in an "*unknown tongue*." It simply means to speak to God. If there is no one present who understands your language, then you are to communicate with God quietly or silently.

We have a brother in our congregation who is from Nigeria. On

September 11, 2001, the day terrorists attacked New York City and the Pentagon, we gathered for prayer. Brother Christopher prayed very intensely – and he prayed in English. If he had prayed in the Nigerian language, no one would have been edified.

If you were to ask him if he ever prays to God in his native language, I am sure he would say "yes," but he prays in his native tongue privately – at home. Or, if he prays in his native tongue at our Church, he prays silently to God.

Nigerian is his native tongue, so which language do you think he would prefer to speak, English or Nigerian?

Obviously, the answer is Nigerian. But on that night following the terrorist attack when we gathered, he prayed aloud in English so the Church could be edified. The Word of God says that only two or three should speak, and then you must have an interpreter.

I once heard a preacher on television say that while onboard a commercial airliner, the Holy Spirit instructed him to speak in "***unknown tongues***" to the passenger next to him.

No way.

A spirit may have instructed him to do so, but it was not the Holy Spirit. Why would a Gentile need to speak to another Gentile in a foreign language when they both speak English?

Paul addresses that matter as follows:

Therefore if I know not the meaning of the voice, I shall be unto him that speaketh a barbarian, and he that speaketh shall be a barbarian unto me. (1 Corinthians 14:11)

What if someone stood up during a service while the choir was ministering and began to sing?

What if someone stood up and said, "I want to preach now," while the pastor was in the middle of his sermon?

This is what must be envisioned as we read 1 Corinthians 14. This is what was actually happening in the Corinthian Church. Worship was absolutely chaotic.

However, the most damage is done when it is required that a

person must speak in "*unknown tongues*" in order to be saved. In Acts 1:14 the disciples prayed while they waited, but it does not say that they prayed for the Holy Ghost to come. They knew He was coming because Jesus had already said to them, "*When I get back to the Father, I will send you another Comforter.*"

Because they believed what Jesus had told them, there was no need for them to pray for the Holy Spirit to come.

Another incident that needs clarification is when the apostles went to Samaria to pray, and to lay hands on the Samaritans so that they could receive the Holy Spirit. This shows that God always has a way of maximizing a bad situation.

I would never suggest that God had a hand in the destruction of the twin towers in New York on September 11, 2001, but God can maximize a bad situation for good purposes. As a result of what happened, there are a lot more people who are calling on Him today than were calling on Him before the tragedy.

So the way God maximized a bad situation in Samaria was to force the apostles to go there and lay hands on the people, and they did. However, the Samaritans did not speak in "*unknown tongues*" because the apostles (Jews) and Samaritans spoke the same language.

There was no delay in receiving the Holy Spirit by the Gentiles at the home of Cornelius. Unlike the disciples in the *Upper Room* who waited and prayed, and unlike the Samaritans who had to wait for the apostles to lay hands on them, in Acts 10:44 the Bible states:

While Peter yet spake these words, the Holy Ghost fell on all them which heard the word.

This is one of the occasions referenced to show that "*tongues*" speaking occurs when people receive the Holy Spirit. However, close scrutiny will show that the Gentiles did not speak in "*unknown tongues*." They spoke "with tongues" (Acts 10:46), which was the sign to the Jews that Gentiles could be saved (Acts 11: 18).

A legitimate question that can be raised is why then, did Paul lay hands on the people at Ephesus? And why did they speak in "*unknown tongues*" as recorded in Acts 19?

The answer is that they were not Christians, were not saved, and had not yet received the Holy Spirit. The narrative says that Paul found certain disciples. It doesn't say that he found Christians. The disciples that he found were disciples of John the Baptist, who had never been brought into the Body of Christ. This is the reason why Paul laid hands on them. That is why they spoke with "*tongues*," thus, providing the Jews another sign that Gentiles could be saved.

Paul began to draw his "correction" epistle to a close with the following words:

If any man think himself to be a prophet, or spiritual, let him acknowledge that the things that I write unto you are the commandments of the Lord. (1 Corinthians 14:37)

In light of all that he said to correct the errors of the Corinthians regarding speaking in "*unknown tongues*," he wanted them to know that all that he said was by commandment of the Lord. In other words, he had authority from God to say what he did. The conclusion is very stern and unapologetic.

But if any man be ignorant, let him be ignorant.
(1 Corinthians 14:38)

Unfortunately, there are many people who believe they have the "gift" to speak in "*unknown tongues*." Nevertheless, the experience of esthetic utterance must be compared to Biblical "*tongues*."

Also, personal opinions must be examined in the light of the Word of God. We have the choice between God's enlightenment and the world's ignorance. Unfortunately, for some people the Word of God is not enough to settle the controversy.

Nonetheless, this makes the words of Paul even more penetrating:

But If any man be ignorant, let him be ignorant.

IV
Miracles and Healings

And by the hands of the apostles were many signs and wonders
wrought among the people; (and they were all with one accord in
Solomon's Porch. And of the rest durst no man join himself to them:
but the people magnified them. And believers were the more added to
the Lord, multitudes both of men and women.) Insomuch that they
brought forth the sick into the streets, and laid them on beds and
couches, that at the least the shadow of Peter passing by might over-
shadow some of them. There came also a multitude out of the cities
round about unto Jerusalem, bringing sick folks, and them which
were vexed with unclean spirits: and they were healed every one.
(Acts 5:12-16)

A Dose of Doctrine

If you are an observant Christian, you are today witnessing an unprecedented attraction to miracles and healings. So-called "healings" are a part of many worship services. However, it becomes our responsibility to compare the attraction of miracles and healings to doctrine that is described in Scripture.

Is the Bible full of miracles?

If you answered "true," you are wrong. The Bible is not full of miracles. It is a mistaken notion to believe that the Bible is a book of miracles. That is an erroneous depiction of the Bible. **In reality, miracles are not as prevalent as most Bible readers may think.**

As with any other theme, miracles and healings must be taken in the Biblical and historical context in which they occur. If this context is ignored, we will reach a false conclusion.

With very little effort and observation, we can see that there is a growing lure to miracles – and, in particular, healing miracles. However, it must be noted that the attraction to healing miracles is not separate and apart from a growing trend in this direction from many pulpits.

Also, numerous authors are writing more and more about these subjects. They both promote and promise miracles to people who have "enough" faith to receive them. One of many titles in the marketplace is **How to Have a Miracle and How to Receive a Miracle.** The subtle and often intimidating emphasis from some pulpits is that you are not a good Christian if you are not expecting and experiencing miracles in your life.

So-called "healing" services are becoming commonplace in worship services today. There are ministers who routinely attempt to perform healings.

This brings to mind a pastor I know who was caught up in the so-called "Faith Movement." He held a "healing" service for his organist who had been diagnosed with cancer. He declared her healed in the name of Jesus. He "named and claimed" her healing. Six weeks later he had to eulogize her.

Miracles and Healings

One morning after the funeral, while at the breakfast table, his children challenged him about her death. They said, "Daddy, you said that God told you that she was healed."

Because of this embarrassing incident, he restructured his theology concerning miracles and healings. He is now trying to repair the damage that he did to the "child-like" faith of his children.

Please consider another true or false question: "Does God still work miracles today?"

"Yes," but it is a qualified "yes." God still works miracles today but not as many in our time as in Biblical times.

Like any other doctrinal matter, what we believe and what we teach about miracles and healings must correspond to the Word of God. A miracle is an act that is caused when the supernatural power of God overrules natural laws in the universe. A miracle occurs when God sets aside the order of a natural law. For example, a miracle occurred when God reversed gravity and made the axe-head swim at the command of Elisha. (2 Kings 6:6)

My observation is that we use the label of a miracle much too loosely. We call many things miracles that simply are not miracles. Unless a natural law has been disturbed, there is no miracle. God can and does intervene in events and circumstances to bless us without disturbing natural laws, but those cases are not miracles. They could better be described as *divine intervention.*

On the other hand, **divine healing occurs when the supernatural power of God intervenes to cure illness and restores health apart from natural means or apart from medical assistance.** Consequently, healings are miracles that do not occur in the environment.

The Performers of Miracles

Who were the performers of miracles in the Old Testament?

You cannot read in the Old Testament very long before you come upon a miracle. The question is: Who were the human personalities that God worked through to bring about miracles in the

Old Testament times?

Only three men: Moses, Elijah and Elisha.

Beyond them – excuse my grammar – "there ain't no more." You won't discover anyone else who performed a miracle other than those three men.

Nevertheless, the fact is that the Old Testament is loaded with men and women of great spiritual capability. There are some "heavy-hitters" who walked across the pages of the Old Testament who never performed a single miracle.

Abraham was one. He is the "father of the faithful," who would have slit his son's throat to offer him as a burnt sacrifice for God.

But, he never worked a miracle.

Isaiah, called the "silver tongue prophet," never worked a miracle.

David, the sweet singer of Israel who expanded the borders of Israel's kingdom beyond what any other king had done or would do, whose accomplishments were the standard for all subsequent kings, never performed a miracle.

Another person, who perhaps should head the list, is Enoch. Enoch walked with God. He lived so close to God that God took him bodily into Heaven. He did not die. Now, with credentials like that, it seems like Enoch would have performed at least one tiny miracle, but he didn't. There is not a single miracle attributed to Enoch.

In the New Testament only Jesus Christ Himself, and His apostles, performed miracles. John, who highlighted only seven of many of the Lord's miracles, wrote:

*And **many other** signs (miracles) truly did Jesus in the presence of His disciples, which are not written in this book.* (John 20:30)

*And there are also **many other things** that Jesus did, the which, if they should be written every one, I suppose that even the world itself could not contain the books that should be written. Amen.*
(John 21:25)

Miracles and Healings

These statements show that the work of Jesus was incomprehensible. He was the foremost performer of miracles. His audience must have gone home dizzy at the end of a day of ministry. John indicates that Jesus performed many more miracles than he included in his book of the Gospels.

Peter referred to the miracles of Jesus in his sermon to the Jews on the Day of Pentecost:

> *"You men of Israel, hear these words, Jesus of Nazareth, a man approved of God among you **by miracles and wonders and signs**, which **God did by Him in the midst of you**, as ye yourselves also know."* (Acts 2:22)

They could not deny the miracles of Jesus, but they would not accept them.

The apostles also performed miracles. The credentials of the apostles are delineated in the following verse:

> *"And these signs shall follow them that believe; in My name shall they cast out devils, they shall speak with new tongues; they shall take up serpents; **and if they drink any deadly thing, it shall not hurt them; they shall lay hands on the sick, and they shall recover**."* (Mark 16:17-18)

These verses describe the **Apostolic Times** of the Church. However, "that was then and this is now." The Apostolic Times, or, **Transitional Period**, was an era when the apostles gave leadership to the Church. We must keep in mind two particular periods when studying the Bible. Simply put, they are **Old Testament Times** and **New Testament Times**.

Another designation of these two times is **Jewish Times** and **Gentile Times**. However, it is critical to understand that the Old Testament era did not end abruptly, nor did the New Testament era begin suddenly.

Notice the distinction of these times:

Not like this...

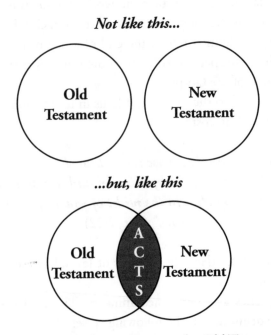

...but, like this

As you can see in the lower diagram, the Old Testament era carried over into the New Testament era. The middle portion represents the time period of the Book of Acts, called the "Apostolic Times" of the Church. This was the time when the apostles gave leadership to the Church.

In the strict sense of the word "Apostle," there are no apostles in the Church today. Jesus said:

*"**And these signs** shall follow them that believe; in my name shall they cast out devils; they shall speak with new tongues."* (Mark 16:17)

*"**Signs**"* were the credentials of an apostle. Signs equate to the miracles they performed through their unique gifts and abilities.

*"**And these signs** shall follow them that believe; in my name shall they cast out devils..."*

On several occasions the apostles exercised demons from possessed people.

"...they shall speak with new tongues." (Not *"**unknown tongues**"*).

People who use Mark 16:17 in an attempt to justify "speaking in tongues" miss the meaning of the verse. It says, "They shall speak with **new tongues**," not *"**unknown" tongues**."* However, for the people who insist that this means speaking in *"**unknown tongues**,"* the application must match the interpretation.

In other words, it means if they can speak in "unknown" tongues, then they ought to be able to drink poison as well.

Nevertheless, Mark 16:17 is not an isolated Scripture. It has its fulfillment in the ministry of the apostle Paul.

*And when Paul had gathered a bundle of sticks, and laid them on the fire, **there came a viper out of the heat, and fastened on his hand**. And when the barbarians saw the venomous beast hang on his hand, they said among themselves, "No doubt this man is a murderer, whom, though he hath escaped the sea, yet vengeance suffereth not to live." **And he shook off the beast into the fire, and felt no harm**. However, they looked when **he should have swollen, or fallen down dead suddenly**: but after they had looked a great while, and saw **no harm come to him**, they changed their minds, and said that he was a god.* (Acts 28:3-6)

The incident when Paul shook the snake off his hand into the fire was another proof of Paul's apostleship. The people on the island expected him to turn green and fall over dead, but he felt no harm. He was an apostle. He had *special protection* from God as an apostle. Not only did the apostles have *special protection* from God, they had *special power* from God. No one today has that kind of protection or power.

The first qualification of an apostle is that he must have received a direct, personal call in the presence of Jesus. The second qualification is that they must have seen the risen Lord. I won't bother to enumerate any other qualifications.

The fact is that there is no one today who can meet those two initial qualifications. In light of the qualifications of an apostle, to think that a person in our time is an apostle is absurd.

It was the Corinthian Church (of all congregations) that raised questions about Paul's apostleship. The Corinthian Church – the folks who got drunk at the Lord's Table, the folks who used sexual improprieties as a form of their worship, the folks who permitted incest to go on in the Church without judging it. They were the ones who wanted to know if Paul was indeed an apostle. They didn't have enough spiritual discernment to know that an authentic apostle was in their midst.

A letter from Paul addressed the issue.

Am I not an apostle? Am I not free? Have I not seen Jesus Christ our Lord? Are not ye my work in the Lord? If I be not an apostle unto others, yet doubtless I am to you: for the seal of mine apostleship are ye in the Lord. Mine answer to them that do examine me is this, have we not power to eat and to drink? Have we not power to lead about a sister, a wife, as well as other apostles, and as the brethren of the Lord, and Cephas? Or I only and Barnabas, have not we power to forbear working? Who goes to warfare any time at his own charges? Who plants a vineyard, and eats not of the fruit thereof? Or who feeds a flock, and eats not of the milk of the flock? Say I these things as a man? Or says not the law the same also? For it is written in the Law of Moses, you shall not muzzle the mouth of the ox that treads out the corn. Doth God take care for oxen? Or says he it altogether for our sakes? For our sakes, no doubt, this is written: that he that plows should plow in hope; and that he that threshes in hope should be partaker of his hope. If we have sown unto you spiritual things, is it a great thing if we shall reap your carnal things? If others be partakers of this power over you, are not we rather? Nevertheless we have not used this power; but suffer all things, lest we should hinder the Gospel of Christ. Do you not know that they that minister about holy things live of the things of the temple? And they that wait at the altar are partakers with the altar? Even so hath the Lord ordained that they which preach the Gospel should live of the Gospel. (1 Corinthians 9:1-14)

He wrote, "*I have the same rights that Cephas has* (he was referring to Peter). *I have a right to escort a sister on my arm, just like Peter.*" Peter had a wife and so could he. But, that was not the only basis for his response. He also said, "*I have the right to forebear working, not because I'm lazy or because I'm too good to work, but because God has ordained that I live off the Gospel.*"

The Corinthian Church would not sustain Paul financially, so he worked (making tents) to provide for himself. Notwithstanding, the most convicting and damaging words in defense of his apostleship, he later wrote to them in the second epistle:

Truly the signs of an apostle were worked among you in all patience, **in signs, and wonders, and mighty deeds**. (2 Corinthians 12:12)

The meaning of those indicting words is that if anyone should have known Paul was an apostle, it should have been the Corinthian Church. After all, they were the "fruit of his Gospel." They had been saved by his preaching.

The apostles were special men, serving in a special time, delivering a special message. In fact, there has never been a time like the Apostolic Times, and those times cannot be replicated.

The early days of the Church were a supernaturally charged time.

Why?

Simple: because the door of opportunity was closing on Israel. Israel was being given the *first* and *last* opportunity to receive the Gospel, based on the Abrahamic Covenant. Paul himself gave the order of priority for the Gospel message.

For I am not ashamed of the Gospel of Christ: for it is the power of God unto salvation to every one that believes; **to the Jew first, and** *also to the Greek* (Gentile). (Romans 1:6)

That was also the order of priority for Jesus. He came unto His own (first) and His own received Him not. This was what was occurring in the period called the Apostolic Times. Israel was the first target group to receive the apostolic message about Jesus Christ. Not only did they reject Christ, they rejected the apostles and their message about Christ as well. Additionally, the apostles' message came attendant by miracles because the Jews were sign seekers.

For **the Jews require a sign**, *and the Greeks seek after wisdom.*
(1 Corinthians 1:22)

Since the Jews wanted signs, God gave them an abundance of indisputable signs.

Insomuch that they brought forth the sick into the streets, and laid them on beds and couches, **that at the least the shadow of Peter passing by might overshadow some of them.** *There came also a multitude out of the cities round about unto Jerusalem, bringing sick folks, and them which were vexed with unclean spirits:* **and they were healed every one.** (Acts 5:15-16)

This dramatically shows the abundance and magnitude of miracles by the apostles during that special time.

When have you ever seen a "healing" service where everyone was healed?

You can stand at the door where a "healing" service is supposed to be taking place and watch people enter sitting in wheelchairs, hobbling on crutches and limping along with their walkers. And, later you will see those same people coming out in the same condition in which they entered.

The times of the apostles are over and cannot be duplicated. They are being imitated by charlatans, but not duplicated.

And God worked **special miracles by the hands of Paul. So that**

Miracles and Healings

from his body was brought unto the sick, handkerchiefs or aprons, and the diseases departed from them, and the evil spirits went out of them. (Acts 19:11-12)

God worked *special miracles* through Paul. Wow! That word "*special*" gives me fits. When I get to Heaven, one of the questions I want answered is, "What is a special miracle?"

How can a miracle be more special than another miracle? Any miracle is special. There are no little miracles or big miracles. It would take the same amount of power to turn water to wine as it would to raise the dead.

If you don't believe it, try it and see which one is easier to do.

What Peter was doing in Jerusalem were "Sesame Street" miracles compared to what Paul was doing in Ephesus. Peter, in comparison to Paul, must have been performing plain ol' vanilla miracles.

God worked special miracles by the hand of Paul. Handkerchiefs from his body were taken to the sick and they were healed. This is where the famous "prayer cloths" originated, but in Paul's case it wasn't a cloth. They were really sweatbands. Paul tied sweatbands around his head when he made tents so the sweat wouldn't run into his eyes.

Somehow, someone apparently touched one of the sweatbands that he had thrown away and was suddenly healed. That is more evidence of the supernatural power that God invested in the apostles, but "that was then and this is now." No one has that kind of miraculous power anymore.

Despite the Gospel message of the apostles that added to the phenomenon of miracles, the Jews still did not believe. This fact answers the viewpoint of people who feel that their faith would be stronger if they could only witness a miracle. A mistaken notion is that we could really live better for the Lord if we could just see one of the miracles that the Bible describes.

That notion is not only mistaken, it's false. It is an absolute certainty that miracles do not increase faith. Despite all the miracles that Jesus performed, the faith of the people was not increased. They simply returned the following day asking Him to do a bigger miracle than the one they had seen the day before. Of all the miracles that Jesus performed, the people still demanded more from Him.

"Show us a sign and we will believe."

Miracles Do Not Increase Faith

Moses approached Pharaoh and announced, *"The Lord said let my people go."*

Following that announcement Pharaoh witnessed miracles 10 times over. One night as he was turning back his bed, frogs leaped out. He sat down the next morning for breakfast and frogs were leaping out of his food. Later on, the Nile River turned into pure blood. The final miracle was the death of the firstborn males in all of Egypt. Pharaoh's own firstborn son died, but he still did not believe. Instead, the Bible says, that he hardened his heart.

Miracles do not increase faith, but this is what does:

Faith comes by hearing, and hearing by the Word of God.
(Romans 10:17)

Faith increases by hearing the Word of God, not by witnessing miracles. It is the Word of God that generates, gravitates and graduates our faith. I am grieved when people won't let the Word of God be sufficient. It grieves me when we won't let the Word of God be all that it was meant to be. The ultimate faith feeder is the Word of God.

I am not "putting down" miracles and healings. I am the recipient of a miracle of healing. I was healed one day while sitting on the examination table in my doctor's office. Through his examination, he had diagnosed a life-threatening problem. Moments later, when he stepped out to speak to the nurse, I bowed my head (sitting naked as a jaybird on that examination table) and prayed, "Lord, take this away. I'm your man, you have my attention; I'll preach your Word."

The doctor scheduled me for a series of test for the following week. When I returned to hear the results, he said to me, "Tim, I don't know what happened. I saw something disturbing last week, but now you're all right."

I didn't attend a "healing" service, no one laid hands on me, and I didn't use a prayer cloth. But, I was healed.

Yes, God still heals in our time, but not as He did in Biblical times.

The purpose for miracles (particularly in the New Testament) was for the sake of Israel. God had made a promise to Abraham and was bound to perform it. Therefore, the Jews were the first in the priority order.

The *Messiah* and the Gospel message by the apostles were presented to them first, and since they were sign seekers, God "pulled out all the stops" for them. For approximately 10 to 15 years, God opened up the floodgates of miracles for Israel. But still, the apostle Paul eventually had to say to Israel, "*From now on, I'm going to the Gentiles and they will hear.*"

Unfortunately, scores upon scores of innocent people in our time are being drawn away and caught up in the phenomenon of the supernatural. It seems like the "fuzzier" something is, the better we like it.

I could use my sweaty hands and be a millionaire in a few months. With a few testimonies from people who were "healed," all I would have to do is declare that the sweat from my hands is "healing" oil and it would be "on" at our Church.

We have all seen it on television, stadiums and arenas packed to capacity with people looking for or expecting a miracle or a physical healing. The shame is, that in their attempts to seek physical healing miracles, some Christians are ignoring the real miracle – the miracle of salvation. Those seeking physical healing miracles allow the real miracle to be overshadowed.

There is no miracle that God can work for you that is more significant than the miracle of your salvation.

There is no miracle that God can perform for me that will

overshadow the miracle of my salvation.

The songwriter was "right on" when he wrote:

It took a miracle to put the moon in space,
It took a miracle to put the stars in place,
But when he saved my soul,
Washed and made me whole,
That was a miracle of love and grace.

Oh yes, by far the most important miracle is our salvation. It was and is a miracle in every sense of the meaning of the word. My goodness, the Bible says that we were dead until we experienced it.

*And you have He **made alive**, who were **dead** in trespasses and sins.* (Ephesians 2:1)

We were dead – dead in trespasses and sins. The last time I checked, when a person is dead and is brought back to life, that is a miracle.

The transition from death to life is a miracle.

What's more, it is *our* miracle.

God is not honored when we reverse His priority by placing excessive importance on something that we should not. That, my friend, is precisely what is being done with the exaggerated interests in physical healings.

According to the Bible, healings were not done for believers. We never see where a Church came together for a "healing service." Miracles were meant to catch the attention of unbelievers so that afterward the message could be preached unto them. The *message* always followed the *miracle*.

You will see that sequence played out throughout the New Testament – and, for that matter, also throughout the Old Testament. At no time did an apostle come to town and announce, "We're having a healing service tonight at Mary's and Martha's house from six-thirty to nine-thirty."

Miracles and Healings

That never happened because miracles were always spontaneous and selective. The ministry of Jesus substantiates this fact.

Now there is at Jerusalem by the sheep market a pool, which is called in the Hebrew tongue Bethesda, having five porches. In these lay a great multitude of impotent folk, of blind, halt, withered, waiting for the moving of the water. For an angel went down at a certain season into the pool, and troubled the water: whosoever then first after the troubling of the water stepped in was made whole of whatsoever disease he had. And a certain man was there, which had an infirmity, thirty and eight years. When Jesus saw him lie, and knew that he had been now a long time in that case, He said to him, "Wilt thou be made whole?" The impotent man answered him, "Sir, I have no man, when the water is troubled, to put me into the pool: but while I am coming, another steps down before me." Jesus said to him, "Rise, take up thy bed, and walk." And immediately the man was made whole, and took up his bed, and walked. (John 5:2-9)

Jesus had come to a place called Bethesda where there were diseases of all varieties. An overabundance of infirmities was represented in the multitude of people. As Jesus walked into the area of mass human suffering, He stepped over someone with lupus, He stepped over someone with cancer, He stepped over someone else with sickle cell anemia, and then He stepped over to a man and asked if he wanted to be made well. After healing the man, He turned around and walked back over the person with lupus, back over the person with cancer, and over the person with sickle cell anemia, to continue on His way.

He healed only one person.

Miracles Were Spontaneous and Selective

Additionally, we must observe that Jesus and the apostles healed without the requirement of faith. *They healed on command.* About the only thing that we have "on command" are the movies on our pay channels.

Jesus healed the man at Bethesda by *divine command*. Even though there were occasions where the Lord required faith for healing, in this case there was none.

The apostles also didn't always require faith. In Acts 3, Peter and John said to a crippled man at the gate of the temple, "*In the name of Jesus of Nazareth take up your bed and walk.*"

They didn't ask him if he had faith. The purpose for mentioning this is so we can see the authority and power of the apostles.

When there is no obvious evidence of a healing, so-called "faith healers" get off the hook by telling people they "didn't have enough faith." This is their loophole for escape. Then they go on to the bank to make their deposit.

Here are some fair questions that should be asked to all alleged faith healers:

A. How much faith does it take for physical healing?

B. How much more faith does it take for physical healing than it takes to be saved?

C. If we had enough faith in God for Him to save us, how much more faith does it take to be healed?

There is an obvious inconsistency in the amount of faith needed for salvation and the amount of faith that "faith healers" are demanding for physical healing. My admonishment to miracle searchers and healing seekers is to save your money. If you never get out of your wheelchair but are saved, you already have the miracle that really matters. If you are saved but you never walk again, you already have the most important miracle of all.

Job knew the difference. He said:

"*And though after my skin worms destroy this body, yet in my flesh shall I see God.*" (Job 19:26)

Job had prioritized his miracles. That's why he could say:

Miracles and Healings

"Though he slay me, yet will I trust in Him." (Job 13:15)

If you have received Jesus Christ as your Savior, you have already received the miracle above all miracles. You have already received God's best miracle – *the permanent miracle.*

No healing miracle is permanent because we will all eventually die or be translated from this body. *Any physical healing miracle is temporary.* However, if your name is written in **The Lamb's Book of Life**, it is there forever.

It is unfortunate that *sensationalism* is drawing many people away from the *simplicity* of Biblical doctrine. Even in our day there are Churches that have "miracle rooms" or "miracle prayer rooms." This is the place where a person can go to claim and wait for a miracle.

The misunderstanding and misappropriation of miracles and healings has grown from the roots of unsound doctrine. Many unsuspecting and innocent souls are victims of the allurement to the illusion of miracles and healings.

When all is said and done, we must return to the Scriptures to identify the performers of miracles. When we do this, we will see that only three men in the Old Testament worked miracles, and that only Jesus and the apostles worked miracles in the New Testament.

It is wise and worth discovering the perimeters of the miracles of Jesus and the apostles. Jesus performed what I call environmental miracles (miracles that occurred in creation) as well as healing miracles. The apostles performed only miracles of healing.

We will be on sound doctrinal footing when we identify the performers of miracles and distinguish between their gifts, power and authority, and why those gifts, power and authority are not invested in men and women today.

The Purpose for Miracles

The purpose of miracles will be a worthwhile "bondage releasing" discovery. Miracles in the Bible can be summarized into four purposes:

A. To display the power of God

B. To direct the attention of the people from the miracle to the message

C. To discern the truth of the message that follows the miracle

D. To discover the authenticity of the messenger

When God called Moses, it was from a burning bush. Moses was herding sheep and minding his own business. One day he walked upon a bush that was burning in the desert but was not being consumed by the flames. The fact that the bush was not burning up quickly got his attention. Moses fixed his *attention* on the burning bush, but soon his *awareness* was turned from the *miracle* to the *message* that he heard. The message from God was, "*Go, tell Pharaoh to let my people go.*"

Every miracle gave birth to a message. When Jesus broke the bread and two fish, He blessed them and passed them to His disciples to give to the multitude. However, while they were eating, the Lord stood up and said, "*I am that bread.*"

He turned their attention from the *miracle* to the *message*. He went on to say, "*I am the bread of life and if you do not eat my body and drink my blood you have no life in you.*"

The Scripture tells us, "*From that time, many of them went back and walked no more with Him.*"

They liked the miracle, but they didn't like the message – nor did they like the messenger to which the miracle pointed.

Peter called the attention of his audience to the miracles of Jesus to authenticate Him and His ministry.

"*Ye men of Israel, hear these words; Jesus of Nazareth, a Man approved by God among you by miracles and wonders and signs, which God did by Him in the midst of you, **as ye yourselves also know**.*" (Acts 2:22)

Miracles and Healings

Nicodemus also authenticated the Lord's ministry:
*The same came to Jesus by night, and said unto him, "**Rabbi, we**
know thou art a teacher come from God: for no man can do
these miracles that thou doest, except God be with him."*
(John 3:2)

In his writings, Paul also referred to his miracles to authenticate
his ministry to the Corinthians:

__Truly the signs of an apostle were wrought among you__
in all patience, in signs, and wonders, and mighty deeds.
(2 Corinthians 12:12)

I challenge Christians to fully understand the purpose for miracles in Biblical times, but the miracle of all miracles is our salvation.
It has already been done *for* us. In fact, it has been done *in* us.

Any physical healing miracle would be the lesser in priority. The
comparison is like trading in a Rolls Royce for a Volkswagen (no
slight intended to people who drive Volkswagens). I'm simply
attempting to show the disproportion of importance to physical
healing over the spiritual healing of salvation.

God had a purpose for the abundance of miracles in Apostolic
Times, and that purpose cannot be duplicated. Please do not be
duped by what cannot be *duplicated.*

The Place for Miracles

The place of miracles is secondary to the word of God. Paul
summarized:

For we walk by faith, not by sight. (2 Corinthians 5:7)

He further addressed the priority of the Word of God.

So then faith cometh by hearing, and hearing by the word of God.

A Dose of Doctrine

(Romans 10:17)

Miracles are sensory. Thus, Paul further admonishes us with these words:

While we look not at the things which are seen, but at the things which are not seen: for the things which are seen are temporal; but the things which are not seen are eternal. (2 Corinthians 4:18)

Our focus should not be upon the things that can be seen, but on what cannot be seen. That certainly sounds contradictory, but by faith we can view things that cannot be seen.

When we apply Paul's words to miracles, it diminishes their worth. Miracles don't have the spiritual value that is often ascribed to them. A classic example is the people of Israel. The spiritual value that they gained from miracles is next to none. They observed an abundance of miracles in Old Testament times as well as in New Testaments times.

Their journey out of Egypt began in the aftermath of a great miracle – sprinkling the blood of a lamb over their doorposts to avoid the touch of the "Angel of Death." But, when they reached the Red Sea they showed that they hadn't gained an ounce of faith from their Passover event.

After witnessing the Red Sea split wide open and walking across it on dry ground, they reached the bitter waters of Marah and proved again that they had not increased their faith from the experience of crossing the Red Sea.

After 40 years of taking fresh breakfast from the leaves each morning, they were still bereft of faith. In fact, they became tired of eating manna and complained to Moses saying, "*We loath this light bread, we want some meat.*"

So, God performed another miracle for them. A covey of quail flew into their camp three feet above the ground, flying in slow motion as if they were drunk.

When have you ever seen birds fly toward people? (Only in Alfred Hitchcock's movie, ***The Birds***.)

Miracles and Healings

Their ingratitude was displayed when they sinned by gorging themselves on the roasted flesh.

The conclusion of their lack of spiritual benefit from observing miracles is as follows:

So we see that they could not enter in because of unbelief.
(Hebrews 3:19)

In New Testament times, they also witnessed an abundance of miracles by Jesus. However, His miracles benefited them very little.

*But though He had done so many miracles before them, **they believed not on Him**.* (John 12:37)

How many miracles did Jesus perform? John said that there were too many to count. If they were written in a book all the books in the world could not contain them. Nevertheless, even though He performed *so many miracles, yet they believe not in Him.*

The miracle of all miracles was the resurrection of the Lord. However, Matthew also shows it did not produce faith.

And when they saw Him, they worshipped Him: but some doubted.
(Matthew 28:17)

Luke records that:

Jesus showed himself alive after the crucifixion by many infallible proofs seen by them for forty days.

However, at the time of His ascension He was worshipped by many "but some doubted."

The miracle of the resurrection had occurred. The Lord stood bodily in their presence. More than 500 people observed Him physically ascend into Heaven and disappear, but some people still doubted.

That's incredible.

However, it only further proves the lesser value of miracles. Israel is the clearest example that little spiritual value can be gained from observing miracles.

Most assuredly, the Bible does not leave us without instruction regarding healing in our time. Notice that the instruction comes from an epistle.

> *Is any among you afflicted? let him pray. Is any merry? let him sing psalms. Is any sick among you? let him call for the elders of the Church; and let them pray over him, anointing him with oil in the name of the Lord: and the prayer of faith shall save the sick, and the Lord shall raise him up; and if he have committed sins, they shall be forgiven him.* (James 5:13-15)

These instructions from James give us permission to pray for ourselves when we are sick. We don't have to call our pastor out of bed in the wee hours of the morning. We ought to be able to pray until dawn for ourselves.

The instructions also include calling for the elders to pray. Notice precisely what the Holy Spirit does here. The instructions are not to call for the apostles.

Why not?

Because the Holy Spirit knew there would be no apostles after the Apostolic Age for the Church to call on. The Holy Ghost knew what He was doing when He inspired James to write these Words. In the coming years when people became sick, there would be no apostles to call upon.

So, whom should you call?

An elder. An elder is equivalent to a pastor, and a pastor is equivalent to a shepherd. All three titles carry the same meaning.

Today a call for the elders means to call the pastor or people from the pastor's staff. The instructions are for the pastor to pray – to pray and anoint with oil in the name of the Lord. It does not say that he is to command healing in the name of Jesus.

Miracles and Healings

Anointing with oil does not mean from a flask of olive oil that is carried in a coat pocket or kept under the pulpit. The interpretation and application of these verses is that it is permissible to utilize the medicinal practices of our time, just as in Biblical days the times dictated using various ointments, oils and salves as medicine. (When I was a boy, I was rubbed down with hog lard and turpentine to break a fever.)

So the instructions are to pray, use the medicinal techniques of our day, but still to pray. This is what James was speaking about. He was not talking about calling people who had assembled for worship down an isle to stand in line to be *zapped*. He wasn't talking about using olive oil from a flask. The anointing was the medical prescriptions of that time, which equals the medical technology of our time.

And the prayer of faith shall save the sick, and the Lord shall raise him up; and if he have committed sins, they shall be forgiven him.
(James 5:15)

This doesn't mean that every sickness is the result of sin. If that were true our Churches would look like the pool of Bethesda on Sunday mornings. Some illnesses are related to sin, but not all illnesses are the result of it.

It is critically essential that we do not lift up miracles out of their secondary place, being mindful that Satan can perform counterfeit miracles that may be mistaken for the real thing. Pharaoh, said to Moses, "Do a miracle for me and I will believe you."

Moses replied, "All right, I have one for you," and he threw down his staff which turned into a snake.

However, Pharaoh's magicians matched Moses "tit for tat" for a while. Pharaoh summoned his magicians and through the trick of optical illusion, they also turned their staffs into snakes.

But, Moses' snake swallowed up their snakes. Therein lies the distinct difference between satanic power and God's power. When Moses took the snake by the tail, it turned back into a staff.

A Dose of Doctrine

Do not be deceived. Satan has supernatural power, but the power of Satan is inferior to the power of God because God has all power. God *creates* with His supernatural power and Satan *counterfeits*. God *performs miracles* and Satan *pretends and mimics*.

The Bible says that Satan disguises himself as an angel of light. Who would he deceive as an angel of darkness? Who would listen to him? In his disguise, Satan counterfeits miracles.

WARNING
Satan's Ability to Counterfeit Spiritual Things Makes Seeking Miracles Extremely Dangerous

Quite simply, nothing worthless is ever counterfeited. When have you heard of anyone serving time in prison for counterfeiting pennies? Satan counterfeits miracles because of the high value that naive people place upon them.

The Book of Revelation is written against the backdrop of a "One-World Religious System" that will be in place at the time of the events that John describes. What will be the catalyst to bring all Churches into one religious system? The answer: simply the division of Christians by denominations.

For example, the Baptist denomination has had difficulty staying in fellowship together. We (National Baptist) have "split" four times since 1912.

What's going to bring us together as one with all the other Christian groups?

The frightening fact is that the thread of deception is already weaving its way into the fabric of every Christian denomination. The stage is being set, right now, for a "One-World Religious System, both inside and outside of the Church. The Anti-Christ will make his appearance to a "One-World Religious System."

Many non-Christians – and also Christians – are being drawn to zodiac and horoscope predictions. There are Christians who can't name the 12 apostles, but have no problem naming the 12 zodiac signs in order. Many times, when single Christians meet for the first time, they barely complete the introductions before they ask each other, "What's your sign?"

There is also a huge growing attraction to psychics by both non-Christians and Christians alike. In Biblical times, God called women psychics "witches" and men psychics "wizards."

Who would have thought that in the United States of America, we would have such a growing interest in the satanic supernatural? We are supposed to be a Christian nation, founded on Christian principles.

I don't know how many times I have heard the words "God Bless America" since September 11, 2001. On our currency is inscribed the words "In God We Trust."

Considering the deep Christian roots of our nation, who would have thought that a witch, calling herself "Miss Cleo," would be able to afford prime-time commercial exposure to display her witchcraft?

Isn't it strange that in a Christian nation a witch can go public, come out of the closet, and openly commercialize witchcraft?

People who don't believe that Jesus could have been born of a virgin, or that God created the Heavens and the earth in six literal days (but rather that it took millions of years to evolve), believe in witchcraft, zodiac signs and other such junk. **The evil behind a "free reading" is the same evil that was behind the bombing of the twin towers on September 11, 2001**. Satan's true intention behind a free reading is his original deceitful plan of destruction of every thing that is good and of God. Jesus personally described Satan's intention.

> *"The thief cometh not, but for to steal, and to kill, and to destroy. I am come that they might have life, and that they might have it more abundantly."* (John 10:10)

This is his ultimate aim behind a free reading, not merely to tell a woman that her husband is cheating on her, and not simply to let a husband know ahead of time that his wife is going to divorce him.

That is not the true intention. The real evil that the Devil wants to perpetrate is to kill, to steal and to destroy.

Satan has sense enough not to appear evil until he is ready to move in with the full payload. However, his deceptiveness is not only taking place outside the Church, but also inside. His evil seeds are being sown at this very moment.

How will the Church become one in theology, having the same belief system?

The seed is being sown with the insistence of newborn Christians – innocent in faith – seeking the phenomenon of so-called "*tongues speaking*." It starts with the gross misrepresentation of the baptism of the Holy Spirit by making it sensory, something a person is supposed to feel, though the Bible says that baptism of the Holy Spirit is when we are placed in the Body of Christ. We can't physically "*feel*" anything, neither do we "*feel*" anything when our name is placed in *The Lamb's Book of Life*.

If we were not familiar with what the Bible teaches, we would not know these truths. Likewise, we would not know the meaning of the baptism of the Holy Spirit.

The attraction to healing services, along with the recent emphasis of being "*slain in the spirit*," is an expansion of the attraction to the supernatural. However, we are not without warning about this growing interest in satanic sensationalism.

Jesus said, "*For there shall arise false Christs, and false prophets, and shall shew great signs and wonders; insomuch that, if it were possible, they shall deceive the very elect*." (Matthew 24:24)

False Christs and false prophets will perform counterfeit miracles. They will show great signs and wonders. The act of being "*slain in the spirit*" appears to be a miracle, but the problem is that there is no reference in the Bible that indicates that the Holy Spirit "*slays*" us. To the contrary, He is the giver of life. In actual fact, we were *dead* in trespasses and in sins and He made us *alive*.

104

Miracles and Healings

The Growing Interest and Attraction to Sensory
Sensationalism Will Serve to Prime People
to Receive the Anti-Christ

And he (Anti-Christ) ***doeth great wonders,*** *so that he maketh fire come down from Heaven on the earth in the sight of men,* ***and deceiveth them that dwell on the earth by the means of those miracles which he had power to do in the sight of the beast;*** *saying to them that dwell on the earth, that they should make an image to the beast, which had the wound by a sword, and did live.*
(Revelation 13:13-14)

Where will he receive the power to do these counterfeit miracles?

...and the dragon gave him his power, and his seat, and great authority. (Revelation 13.2)

The Anti-Christ will come to a people who are already primed for sensational phenomena through zodiac, psychics, so-called "faith healers," and through the teachings that force people to accept sensory experiences as their "evidence." Innocent, ignorant and unsuspecting people will be primed for Satan's payload, and he will be more than pleased to deliver. Even more frightening is that he will nearly deceive the elect of God.

What shall be the anchor that will hold Christians in the midst of this ferocious storm of spiritual illusion? What will keep Christians from being deceived?

The answer is *knowledge of the Word of God, and placing our full assurance in it.*

God's Word is the true ultimate test for the authenticity of miracles and healings. Whatever may appear to be the work of God must match with the Word of God irrespective of its sensational magnitude.

Finally, if we completely trust in the Word of God for our assur-

105

ance of salvation we will have the best confirmation that we already possess all that God has promised. This assurance keeps us from the *feeling* of being incomplete and stems the desire to seek for any extra-Biblical experience for our security. God's Word tell us all our sins are covered by the blood of Jesus, and that our names are in ***The Lamb's Book of Life***.

Furthermore, we presently are seated in Heavenly places. All the assurance and confirmation we need is in the Word of God. *No miracle or healing exceeds our salvation miracle.* The miracle of all miracles has been performed in us, we have the greatest of all miracles; the eternal salvation of our souls, and the confirmation is God's Word.

V
Understanding Salvation

Brethren, my heart's desire and prayer to God for Israel is, that they might be saved. For I bear them record that they have a zeal for God, but not according to knowledge. For they being ignorant of God's righteousness, and going about to establish their own righteousness, have not submitted themselves unto the righteousness of God. For Christ is the end of the law for righteousness to every one that believeth. For Moses describeth the righteousness which is of the law, that the man which doeth those things shall live by them. But the righteousness which is of faith speaketh on this wise, Say not in thine heart, Who shall ascend into Heaven? (that is, to bring Christ down from above:) or, Who will descend into the deep? (that is, to bring up Christ again from the dead.) But what saith it? The word is nigh

thee, even in thy mouth, and in thy heart: that is, the word of faith,
which we preach; that if thou shalt confess with thy mouth the Lord
Jesus, and shalt believe in thine heart that God hath raised Him from
the dead, thou shalt be saved. For with the heart man believeth unto
righteousness; and with the mouth confession is made unto salvation.
For the Scripture saith, Whosoever believeth on Him shall not be
ashamed. For there is no difference between Jew and Greek: for the
same Lord over all is rich unto all that call upon Him. For whosoever
shall call upon the name of the Lord shall be saved.
(Romans 10:1-13)

Needless to say, much confusion and contradiction surrounds the matter of salvation and extends to how a person is saved. We often hear various and sundry ways to be saved – not only how, but who can be saved, or who is saved. Some people actually declare some saved people to be "unsaved." It is a presumptuous allegation that is primarily made by people who base their understanding on something other than by God's grace alone.

It is not only a matter of *who* and *how*, but when are we saved. Some declare that salvation is not secure unless a person stays holy until the day he dies.

How can a person know for sure that they are saved? What is the evidence?

The fact is that God has spoken clearly on the matter of salvation. The problem, however, is with our understanding and accepting the clear teaching of God's Word regarding salvation. The problem is further exaggerated when we approach the subject with personal preferences and viewpoints – and, unfortunately, some people are victims of denominational viewpoints.

I am not trying to present a Baptist viewpoint of salvation. I can see clearly when my denominational viewpoints clash with the Word of God. I am not ashamed, nor am I too proud to admit that there are areas where my denomination's viewpoints clash with the Word of God. However, I am forced and obligated to accept God's Word as the final answer and authority.

Understanding Salvation

The first "Declaration of Faith" by the Baptist Church states:

We believe that the Holy Bible was written by men who were divinely inspired, and is a perfect treasure of Heavenly instruction; that it has God for its author, salvation for its end, and truth without any mixture of error for its matter; that it reveals the principles by which God will judge us; and therefore is, and shall remain to the end of the world the true center of Christian union, and the supreme standard by which all human conduct, creeds, and opinions should be tried.

Simply put, the Word of God is the first and only source of authority over anyone, anything and everything. My personal conviction is to uphold the revealed Word of God irrespective of denominational viewpoints. In previous generations there were preachments by my (Baptist) forefathers that I will not and cannot repeat. Not even holding a gun to my head could make me say that you have to be a Baptist to go to Heaven. I would die first.

If that were true, how was God saving people before the Baptists were in business? How was God saving people before the Pentecostals were started? How was God saving people before the Church of God in Christ congregations came on the scene?

By grace through faith in Jesus Christ, that's how.

Either we are saved or we are not. Either we will spend eternity in the presence of God, or we will spend it in hell with fire and brimstone.

A lot of people don't want a Gospel that includes fire and brimstone. They want a "soft and easy Gospel." However, whoever has not accepted Christ will receive fire and brimstone.

Someone once said, "It is better to believe that there is a Heaven and hell, and when you die discover that it's *not true*, than to believe there is *no* Heaven and hell, and when you die discover that *it's true*."

I recall some years ago when the Russian cosmonauts achieved the first space walk, beating us to it. The Russians were ahead of us in the "space race."

When the press interviewed them, the first thing one of them

109

said was, "I didn't see God out there."

The entire room broke up in laughter. But, I'll bet that if he had taken off his spacesuit out there, he would have seen God.

The Problem

There is a problem that connects to the matter of salvation. It is a one-word problem, and only three letters: S-I-N. I learned early as a boy that you couldn't spell "sin" without saying "I."

According to Genesis 3, an incident occurred in the Garden of Eden that brought sin into the human bloodline – the incident of Adam and Eve. We used to call it "the sin of Adam," but nowadays we must upgrade and call it "the sin of Adam *and* Eve." They both ate fruit that God forbade them to eat.

There is a lot of speculation as to what kind of fruit it was. I tried to figure it for many years, and then was given the answer by the Holy Ghost. It was *forbidden fruit*, that's what kind it was – *forbidden fruit*. That's what made it a sin. There was nothing mystical about it. It was sinful for them to eat simply because God instructed them not to.

Paul's epistemic summary was written against the backdrop of our fallen fore-parents in the Garden.

*Wherefore, as **by one man sin entered into the world**, and **death by sin**; and **so death passed upon all men**, for that all have sinned.* (Romans 5:12)

The same scene inspired David's confession.

Behold, I was shapen in iniquity; and in sin did my mother conceive me. (Psalm 51:5)

Paul's writing reveals that *death is the main evidence of sin*. Everything that lives dies, whether animate and inanimate. Adultery is not the main evidence of sin, nor is thievery or robbery. Even murder is not the main evidence of sin. The main evidence of sin is death.

The wages of sin is death.

If you know someone who claims to be sinless, the only way it can be proven is for the person not to die. When that person is rolled down the aisle we can say, "Peek-a-boo, you too."

The wages of sin is death.

Sin separates us from God. Therefore sin must be dealt with so we can have a right relationship with Him. The theological term is "eradicated." Sin must be eradicated – and only the blood of Jesus Christ can accomplish the removal of sin.

*And every priest standeth daily ministering and offering oftentimes the same sacrifices, which can never take away sins; but this man, **after he had offered one sacrifice for sins for ever, sat down on the right hand of God**. (Hebrews 10:11,12)*

Think about that old song:

What can wash away my sin?
The answer is:
Nothing but the blood of Jesus.
What can make me whole again?
Same answer:
Nothing but the blood of Jesus.

So the problem that must be conquered is sin. Your sin and my sin will block us from a righteous standing with God unless our sin is removed.

The Provision

There is only one exclusive provision for our salvation, and that is Jesus Christ. There is no other name whereby we can be saved except by the name of Jesus. The blood of Jesus Christ cleanses us from all our sin. The provision for our sin and salvation is Jesus Christ.

It is enlightening to know that our provision for salvation was not an afterthought by God.

For we which have believed do enter into rest, as He said, "As I have sworn in my wrath, if they shall enter into my rest; *although the works were finished from the foundation of the world*." (Hebrews 4:3)

*And all that dwell upon the earth shall worship him, whose names are not written in the book of life of **the Lamb slain from the foundation of the world***. (Revelation 13:8)

This means that God was not surprised by the sin of Adam and Eve. It also means that the provision for our salvation was not an afterthought by God. In the mind of God, Jesus died before God created anything. God is omniscient: God knows all and has all wisdom. Knowing that Adam and Eve would sin, God made the provision before they fell.

God never plays catch up to Satan.

The provision for salvation is Christ's *vicarious* death and *victorious* resurrection. Jesus was, and is, the complete fulfillment of the analogy of the Old Testament's sacrificial lamb. The analogy is that during that time lambs, heifers and doves were sacrificed for sin. Jesus Christ, however, is the *literal, actual, absolute fulfillment* of that Old Testament's analogy.

John 18:37 records the testimony Jesus gave to Pilate concerning His inevitable death: "*To this end was I born, and for this cause came I into the world.*"

When he was returned to stand before Pilate for the final "trial," Pilate said to Him, "*Know you not that I have power to crucify you and power to release you?*"

However, before Pilate made that arrogant statement, Jesus had previously spoken about His death to His disciples. He said to them, *"Therefore, my Father loves me, because I lay down my life that I may take it again. No man takes it from me, but I lay it down of myself. I have power to lay it down, and I have power to take it again."* Jesus gave His life freely and voluntarily.

The Perquisite

The discovery of the perquisite comes from the clearest verse in the Bible that also reveals the provision for our salvation.

That if thou shalt confess with thy mouth the Lord Jesus, and shall believe in thine heart that God hath raised Him from the dead, thou shalt be saved. (Romans 10:9)

I realize that we typically prefer John 3:16 as the main salvation verse. I love John 3:16, too. Most Christians can rattle it off without a conscious effort, or when half asleep.

For God so loved the world, that He gave His only begotten son, that whosoever believeth in Him should not perish, but have everlasting life.

A person can be saved by this verse, but as a theological verse it lacks the definitive clarity of Romans 10:9.

Another excellent "salvation verse" is Ephesians 2:8-9.

For by grace are ye saved through faith; and that not of yourselves: it is the gift of God: not of works, lest any man should boast.

As precious as this Scripture is with its preferential insinuation to grace over works, we must turn to Romans 10:9 for the absolute criteria of belief for salvation. This Scripture has clarity because of its *practicality*. It is so clear, so simplistic, that some people refuse it and reject it with the explanation that its content can only result in initial salvation. The teaching by some is that the initial salvation that is received from this Scripture must be followed up by salvation *"in its fullness with the evidence of speaking in tongues (**unknown tongues**)."*

Any traditional viewpoint that anyone may hold about salvation is blown away by Romans 10:9. It also blows away any *preferred denominational viewpoint* that suggests Romans 10:9 is a Jewish verse, and that Gentiles should not use it. I am absolutely astounded by the thought that anyone could make such a conclusion – that Jews are saved by Romans 10:9, and that we are saved by some other criteria.

Not only is that ridiculous, it is wrong.

The epistle to the Romans is the clearest dissertation of Christian theology in the New Testament. To insinuate that it is exclusively for the Jews challenges the integrity and the veracity of the Holy Spirit. We can settle whom it was written *for* by identifying whom it was written *to*.

It was addressed to the Church at Rome. Paul did not establish this Church, nor had he ever visited it. We draw that conclusion from his own words in the salutation where he writes, *"I long to see you."*

The Roman Church was not a Jewish Church. The Jerusalem Church was the only predominately Jewish Church. Consequently' Paul was not writing to Jews. Consider the following Scripture:

*Now I would not have you ignorant, brethren, that oftentimes I purposed to come unto you, (but was let hitherto) that I might have some fruit among you also, **even as among other Gentiles**.*
(Romans 1:13)

At the time this epistle was written, the "door of opportunity" was either closed or closing for the Jews. Further proof that he was writing to Gentiles is found in the following Scripture:

*For I could wish that myself were accursed from Christ for **my brethren, my kinsmen according to the flesh**.* (Romans 9:3)

Understanding Salvation

It is not difficult to determine if that statement was written in reference to the Jews. While writing to this Gentile Church, he simply makes a reference about his "kinsmen."

Brethren, my heart s desire and prayer to God for Israel is, that they may be saved. For I bear them record that they have a zeal of God, but not according to knowledge. For they being ignorant of God s righteousness, and going about to establish their own righteousness, have not submitted themselves unto the righteousness of God.
(Romans 10:1-3)

If this epistle were for the Jews, why would Paul write to them in third person?

References to Israel only show that Paul never lost his personal desire for the salvation of his people. If you had 10 children and nine of them were saved wouldn't your heart's desire be that the one lost child would be saved? That's the meaning of the first verse.

In Romans 10:8-9, he went from third person to second person:

*The word is nigh **thee**, even **thy mouth**, and in **your heart**: that is, the word of faith, which we preach; that if thou shalt confess with **thy mouth** the Lord Jesus, and shalt believe in **thine heart** that God hath raised Him from the dead, thou shalt be saved.*

As Paul moved from third person to second person, we see clearly who is the target of his letter.

The English word, "confess" is translatable into the Greek compound word "*homologeo.*" "*Homo*" means "*same.*" "*Logeo*" comes from the word "*logos,*" which means "*words.*"

When we confess, we must say the same words about Jesus that God has said.

We must confess that Jesus is Lord.

Confessing is the same thing as an admission. When someone confesses to a crime, it is an admission. We must admit that Jesus is who God says He is, and God says, "***He is Lord.**"*

This perquisite is twofold.

One, it is to **confess that Jesus is Lord**. Cults do not believe Jesus is God. This is how we know it is a cult. This separates the "*saints*" from the "*aints.*"

In the first area of the prerequisite we are to **confess** or **admit** that **Jesus is Lord**. He is the one and only true God-man, God in the flesh, who took on the form of a servant. He humbled Himself and became obedient unto death, even the death of the cross.

We must confess, saying the same words (*homologeo*) that God says about Jesus. Matthew 22:44 is a quote directly from Psalm 110:1 where David "*in the Spirit*" called the Son of David, Lord:

> *"The Lord said unto my Lord, 'Sit thou at my right hand, until I make thine enemies thy footstool.'"*

This is *homologeo*.

The second fold of the perquisite is introduced by a great big "*AND.*"

"***And believe*** *in your heart.*"

This doesn't mean your blood pump. Our blood pump is not what does the believing. "Heart" more directly means "spirit." Accepting spiritual truths is a spiritual venture. We must believe something specific to have our sins rolled away and be placed into a right relationship with God. There are a lot of things in the Bible that we must believe, but we need to believe only one specific detail for salvation.

We must believe everything the Bible says, but believing everything the Bible says still won't save us.

I believe God created the universe in six literal days, but believing that won't save me.

I believe Noah built an ark and floated it upon the water for a whole year, but believing that won't save me.

I believe Jesus walked on the Sea of Galilee in the midst of a storm, but believing that won't save me.

There is something specific that we must believe for salvation, something at the center of the target that we must hit with our arrow of belief. **We must believe in our heart that God raised Jesus from the dead**. When we believe this, we will be saved.

First is the confession that **Jesus is Lord**.

Next is to **believe the resurrection of Jesus**.

And, the Bible says, "*You shall be saved.*"

"*Shall*" is a declaration in consequence of our belief. It is not a designation of a future time element. People reject the reality of present tense salvation and try to make "*shall*" a future designation of salvation based on our behavior. Our salvation is not based on our behavior to be saved, and it is not based on our behavior to remain saved.

I have a friend who says that when "God says '*Shall*,' He's shooting with a loaded gun."

*Surely goodness and mercy **shall** follow me all the days of my life: and I will dwell in the house of the Lord for ever.* (Psalm 23:6)

*Fret not thyself because of evildoers, neither be thou envious against the workers of iniquity. For they **shall** soon be cut down like the grass, and wither as the green herb.* (Psalm 37:1,2)

*For the Lord Himself **shall** descend from Heaven with a shout, with the voice of the archangel, and with the trump of God: and the dead in Christ **shall** rise first.* (1 Thessalonians 4:16)

It is strange that we can accept the meaning of "*shall*" in other Scriptures, but have so much difficulty with it in Romans 10:9.

It is God's declaration. Believe it and receive it.

The Proof

Many Christians struggle with the proof of their salvation. Simply stated, the proof is the Word of God.

Who declares us saved when we confess that **Jesus is Lord** and believe in our hearts that God raised Him from the dead?

God does.

No one can declare you *unsaved* when God has declared you *saved* according to His Word. We must go *from feeling, to faith, to fact*. Sometimes we may not always feel saved. After all, sometimes I feel like a million dollars, but that's just a feeling.

Airplane pilots experience something called vertigo (not only airplane pilots, anyone can have vertigo). This is when the inner ear malfunctions and you lose your equilibrium. When pilots experience vertigo in flight, they feel as if the airplane is upside down.

What are the key words?

"Feel like."

Pilots are taught in flight training that if they ever experience vertigo in flight, they are to immediately call the air traffic controller.

For example, Pilot Jones is flying his plane 37,000 feet high at 600 miles an hour when he begins to experience vertigo. He calls the air traffic controller and says, "This is pilot Jones, and I'm experiencing vertigo. I feel like my plane is upside down."

The air traffic controller comes back and says, "Pilot Jones, I read you loud and clear. Now, look at your instrument panel."

Pilot Jones looks at his instrument panel, which indicates that the plane is straight. At that moment Pilot Jones has a choice; he can fly the plane based on his feeling, or he can fly it based on the instrument panel.

If you were pilot Jones, which would you choose to do?

I hope you would choose the instrument panel.

Unfortunately, in some cases the feeling is so strong that the pilot adjusts the plane to accommodate his feeling. Now the plane is upside down for real, which often results in the plane crashing.

This is what allegedly happened to John Kennedy Jr. He was an inexperienced pilot who would not depend on his instrument panel. Consequently, he flew his plane straight into a lake.

The news often records stories of fighter pilots who fly their planes straight into the ground. When I see something like that on

TV, I feel like yelling cut to the pilot through the television screen, "Just pull up on the stick, man." But, if a pilot is disoriented in space, confused by his feelings, he often will not rely on his instrument panel.

There will be times, certainly, when you won't feel saved because you know you are unworthy of your salvation. You know you are not worthy and the devil knows that you know you are not worthy. This is when he moves in with all of his deceptive disorientation. He can run you straight out of the Church and back into the world. However, if you will depend on your instrument panel, which is the Word of God, you can *reconfirm* your salvation over and over again.

Understanding salvation can be confusing and complicated, to say the least, but it is not necessary that it be confusing and complicated – because God's Word is very clear about the *criteria* and the *confirmation*. Be sure to always use God's Word for your assurance. Then you can joyfully recite the testimony of the Psalmist.

For ever, O Lord, Thy Word is settled in Heaven. (Psalm 119:89)

VI
What is the Anointing?

And this I say, lest any man should beguile you with enticing words.
Beware lest any man spoil you through philosophy and vain deceit,
after the tradition of men, after the rudiments of the world, and not
after Christ. (Colossians 2:4,8)

Sound doctrine is critical for Christians and the basis for true discipleship. False teaching is the subversive attack of Satan on the Word of God. In fact, the first work of Satan was an attack on the integrity of God's Word. God had told Adam and Eve not to eat of a certain tree in the Garden of Eden, but Satan's question to Eve essentially meant, "Did God really say that?"

The first time that we see Satan in Scripture, he's undermining the Word of God.

If you have ever had your words twisted out of their original meaning, you know how it feels. To have your words misquoted is like having someone steal something from you. This is precisely what Satan does with God's Word. He twists, turns and undermines it until it no longer resembles what God has said.

False teachers do the same thing.

All you have to do is turn on your television or radio and you will hear the loose meaning and application of the word "*anointing*." It is being marketed as the "*cure-all*" for spiritually ailing Christians.

If you are having a "*lethargic moment*" in your Christian walk, you will be told that you need the "*anointing*."

If you are in a ministry that is not thriving, that is faltering or failing, you will be told that you need the "*anointing*."

When a person has delivered a good speech or talk, most likely the explanation will be that they were speaking under the "*anointing*." It is common to say that a person sings with the "*anointing*."

What is the anointing?

More specifically, what is the anointing of the Holy Ghost?

The ministry of the Holy Spirit is receiving more attention now than at any other time in the history of the Church. At times the Holy Spirit is recognized to the exclusion of the ministry and work of Jesus Christ. It is not unusual to hear people attribute to the Holy Spirit work that has been done by Jesus Christ.

Years ago there was a popular song with the following lyrics:

The Holy Ghost saved me.
The Holy Ghost set me free.
I'm just talking about the Holy Ghost.

The truth is, the Holy Ghost did not save us. Jesus is the Savior. The Holy Spirit's ministry is to keep (seal) them whom the Lord has saved.

In many instances the ministry of the Holy Spirit is being grossly exaggerated and distorted. An un-Biblical viewpoint of the ministry of the Holy Spirit is being alleged in our time on a large scale to an unsuspecting audience. This exaggerated view of the ministry of the Holy Spirit takes extreme personal liberties in interpreting the Word of God, violating a warning given in Scripture.

*Knowing this first, that no prophecy of the Scripture is of **any private interpretation**.* (2 Peter 1:20)

We should not make up definitions without regard for the Word of God, nor should we give interpretations without regard for the Word of God. Sadly, some of the most prominent ministers of our time have popularized the prevalent emphasis on the anointing of the Holy Spirit.

It's commonly called *"the anointing."*

The misinterpretation of *"the anointing"* is spilling over into evangelical denominations. We pick up words, phrases and slogans here and there that we have not run through the filter of God's Word. The popular interpretation for *"the anointing"* does not have any Biblical connection at all.

To arrive at the meaning of the *"the anointing,"* we must first consider the general meaning. In the rules of Biblical interpretation, called *"Hermeneutics,"* there is a rule known as **"The Law of First Mention."** The sure way to arrive at the bare essence of the meaning of an act, procedure or a single word in the Bible is to observe it in its first appearance in Scripture. The word *"anoint"* appears for the first time in the Old Testament.

*"And thou shalt put them upon Aaron thy brother, and his sons with him; and shalt **anoint** them, and **consecrate** them, and **sanctify** them, that they may minister unto me in the priest's office."* (Exodus 28:41)

In the initiation of the priesthood, God instructed Moses to *"anoint"* Aaron and his sons. The basic meaning of *"anoint"* is to externally douse, pour or drench a person or an object. It was also done by rubbing or massaging salve or ointment. The common liquid for anointing was oil. Oil is one of the main symbols for the Holy Spirit.

In the case mentioned in Exodus 28:41, the "*anointing*" of Aaron and his sons was accomplished by pouring oil upon them by Moses. God said to Moses, "*Anoint them and consecrate them.*" The word "*consecrate*" is translated from the Hebrew word "*male.*" This is the same word that is used as "*fill*" in Genesis.

And God blessed them, and God said unto them, "Be fruitful, and multiply, and replenish (fill) the earth, and subdue it: and have dominion over the fish of the sea, and over the fowl of the air, and over every living thing that moveth upon the earth." (Genesis 1:28)

"*Male*" can be translated to mean *fill, accomplish* or *prepare.* The meaning in Exodus 28:41 is to "*prepare.*" Moses prepared them by pouring oil over them.

Consequently, **consecration is a form of preparation**. A big part of consecration is prayer. In many Churches there is a "*consecration time*" prior to worship. This is when the congregation is led in special prayer time for preparation of worship.

Specifically, the Lord told Moses to "*consecrate*" (prepare) them, and "*sanctify*" them. The Hebrew word for "*sanctify*" is "*kodesh.*" This means to "*hallow*" or "*separate.*"

The basic meaning of "*sanctify*" is **to be set aside for service unto God**.

From Exodus 28:41 we have the first mention of the word "*anoint.*" We get the first meaning (a twofold meaning) of "*consecrate*" (prepare) and to "*sanctify*" by setting apart. In this case, they were set apart to do the ministry of the priest office unto the Lord. The "*anointing*" was *symbolically accomplished* by pouring oil upon Aaron and his sons.

In the New Testament the first time the word "anoint" appears in connection with service unto God is in Luke 4:18. These are the

What is the Anointing

Words of the Lord as He stood in the temple to announce the beginning of His public ministry:

"The Spirit of the Lord is upon Me, because He hath anointed Me to preach the Gospel to the poor; He hath sent Me to heal the broken-hearted, to preach deliverance to the captives, and recovering of sight to the blind, to set at liberty them that are bruised."

Notice that the Lord **did not say**, "The Spirit of the Lord is in me." Even though the Lord's announcement is recorded in a New Testament book of the Bible, He had the Old Testament external anointing: "The Spirit was upon Him."

The meaning of "*anointed*" is that He was "*consecrated*" (set aside) **to begin His ministry of reconciliation and redemption**.

Another New Testament Scripture in which Jesus clarifies the use of the word "*anoint*" is in Matthew 6:17:

*"But thou, when thou fastest, **anoint** thine head, and wash thy face."*

Jesus taught that people should "***anoint***" (wash) themselves when they were fasting. The custom of those days was not to bathe, trim beards or comb one's hair so it would be known that they were fasting. However, the Lord taught them to groom themselves when they were fasting. The washing and grooming was "***anointing***."

Another meaning is found in the following Scripture:

*And when the Sabbath was past, Mary Magdalene, and Mary the mother of James, and Salome, had brought sweet spices that they might come and **anoint** Him.* (Mark 16:1)

This was when the women went to the tomb to "***anoint***" the Lord's body. They did not have the opportunity to completely "embalm" Him before He was placed in the tomb.

Jesus also speaks of "***anointing***" in Luke 7:46:

*"Mine head with oil thou didst not **anoint**: but this woman hath anointed my feet with ointment."*

This was the occasion when Jesus rebuked Simon, His dinner host, who had not properly welcomed Him to his home. Simon had not provided Him the customary refreshments, water to wash His feet and hands, and scented oil for His hair.

The word "*anoint*" appears several times in Scripture, each time with a specific meaning. In Luke 4:18, "*anointing*" was for service unto God:

*"The Spirit of the Lord is **upon** Me."*

The Old Testament ministry of the Holy Spirit is distinguishable from the New Testament ministry by the fact that the Spirit was *upon* Him. We must recognize that Jesus lived in submission to the time of the Old Testament Jewish laws, which included the ministry of the Holy Spirit.

*But when the fullness of the time was come, God sent forth his Son, made of a woman, **made under the law**.* (Galatians 4:4)

Jesus lived, ministered and died under the old dispensation of the Law. He was submissive to the customs and practices of that day.

"As His custom was, He would go into the synagogue to worship on the Sabbath Day."

The ministry of the Holy Spirit was the same in Jesus' time as it was in Old Testament times. The ministry of Jesus took place in the Old Testament era even though it appears in the New Testament. That's why the text says, "*The Spirit of the Lord is **upon** Me.*" The Holy Spirit performed an external ministry in Old Testament times.

What is the Anointing

The New Testament dispensation did not begin until "*the Day of Pentecost was fully come.*" Pentecost began the **Church Age** or **Church Dispensation** and ushered in a different style of ministry by the Holy Spirit.

The distinction for the ministry of the Holy Spirit in New Testament times is that He ministered inwardly. The indwelling ministry by the Holy Spirit began in New Testament times and is His present ministry to the people of God.

Let us be careful not to overlook the basic meaning of Luke 4:18, which was that Jesus was "***anointed***" (consecrated) to begin His ministry of redemption.

Two other Scriptures mention the "***anointing***" of Jesus.

"For of a truth against thy holy child, Jesus, whom thou hast anointed, both Herod, and Pontius Pilate, with the Gentiles and the people of Israel, were gathered together." (Acts 4:27)

*"How God **anointed** Jesus of Nazareth with the Holy Ghost and with power; Who went about doing good, and healing all who were oppressed of the devil; for God was with Him."* (Acts 10:38)

The clear and distinctly different meanings of "***anointed***" in both of these references are given by simply reading the text. One refers to Christ's death, the other to His ministry.

The main purpose of this chapter is to show the Biblical usage of "**anointing**" for Christians. **There are only three references to the "anointing" of the Holy Spirit for Christians**.

Now He which stablisheth us with you in Christ, and hath anointed us, is God. (2 Corinthians 1:21)

But ye have an unction (anointing) from the Holy One, and ye know all things. (1 John 2:20)

*But the **anointing** which ye have received from Him abideth in you* (not "upon" you), *and ye need not that any man teach you* (this means you do not need a false teacher): *but as the same* **anointing** *teacheth you concerning all things, and is truth, and is no lie, and even as it hath taught you, ye shall abide in Him.* (1 John 2:27)

The aforementioned Scriptures show that the anointing of the Holy Spirit is a present tense occurrence. The "**anointing**" is not something that a person has to *seek, pursue* or *pray* to receive.

It is commonly, (but un-Biblically) taught that a Christian must maintain a high spiritual quality lifestyle in order to "keep the **anointing**," or not to "lose the **anointing**." This teaching is usual-ly translated into something such as: "After you have *strained* and *grunted, prayed* and *agonized, moaned* and *groaned,* you will finally receive it. Then you have the responsibility to *strain* and *agonize* and *groan* and *moan* in order to maintain it."

This is the common meaning of "the **anointing** ministry" of the Holy Spirit. However, the Biblical meaning given in the Scripture says, "*He is in you, and* **abides in you**."

The "**anointing** of the Holy Spirit" is *internal not external.* A correct interpretation of these verses will show that the "**anointing** of the Holy Spirit" is not reserved for a select few, special or spiritu-al Christians. The "**anointing** of the Holy Spirit" *is not selective; it is collective.* **All Christians have "the anointing."**

In 2 Corinthians 1:21, the entire Corinthian Church had received the "**anointing** of the Holy Spirit."

Now he who establishes us with you (plural) *in Christ, and has* **anointed us** *is God.*

Paul spoke of the "**anointing**" to include the entire Corinthian Church, not just certain people. There is no teaching in the Bible to the effect that some Christians have "**the anointing**" and other Christians do not. If you are saved, you have "**the anointing of the Holy Spirit**."

The Corinthian epistle was written to the collective body of believers. Whoever reads the epistle is included in the term, "*has anointed us*."

Both Scriptures mentioned earlier from the epistle of John refer to "*the anointing*" in the present tense.

The "*anointing of the Holy Spirit*" is actually confused with the "filling of the Spirit." It's like calling a Cadillac a Ford. You can't call a Cadillac a Ford, no matter how well meaning your intentions may be. It's like using the word "*is*" when you should be using "*are*."

At times my father had difficulty with these two verbs. He was a good man with a good heart – a deacon until he died. He would give you the shirt off of his back. But, that didn't make him right when he interchanged these two words. It is simply not right to use the word "is" when you should be using the word "are" – period.

Likewise, we cannot arbitrarily impose our own meaning on the different ministries of the Holy Spirit. It doesn't matter how good your heart is. It doesn't matter how good someone's intentions are. We must not confuse the "*filling of the Spirit*" with the "*anointing of the Holy Spirit*." On the other hand, we must not call the "*anointing of the Holy Spirit*" the "*filling of the Holy Spirit*." They are not the same, just as a Cadillac is not a Ford.

The "*anointing of the Holy Spirit*" is for *consecration, preparation* and *sanctification* – to be set apart for service. The "*anointing of the Spirit*" designates *the privilege to serve*. The "*filling of the Spirit*" demonstrates *the power to serve*.

At the time when David was anointed King of Israel, he was also designated to the position of King. The "*anointing of the Holy Spirit*" is like that; it gives us *the privilege to serve*, but the "*filling*" gives us *the power to serve*.

And they were all filled with the Holy Ghost, and began to speak with other tongues, as the Spirit gave them utterance. (Acts 2:4)

This verse refers to the Day of Pentecost. Pentecost was the beginning of the New Testament dispensation. The difference is that in the Old Testament the work of the Holy Spirit was *external*.

In New Testament times His work is *internal*. This is evident by the fact that the disciples were **filled**. Every time we see the words "***filling of the Spirit***" in the Scripture, it will be followed by some act or performance of ministry. In this case, the enabling provided by the "**filling**" was that they all began to speak with "***other tongues***," meaning other languages, not "***unknown tongues***," which was a unique problem in the Corinthian Church.

Then Peter, filled with the Holy Ghost, said unto them...

This prefaces the sermon that Peter preached to the Jewish people on the Day of Pentecost. According to Acts 4:8, some of them were "*rulers of the people and elders of Israel.*" This indicates that Peter preached to some of the men who were responsible for crucifying Jesus. The filling of the Spirit provided the boldness that enabled him to preach.

And when they had prayed, the place was shaken where they were assembled together; and they were all filled with the Holy Ghost, and they spake the word of God with boldness. (Acts 4:31)

Acts 4 records another time when they were assembled together and were "**filled**." This time the "**filling**" was for boldness. Whenever there is "**filling**" by the Holy Spirit, it enables people for service. In addition to the question raised in the overall theme, the conclusion will consist of answering four questions:

1. Who has the anointing of the Holy Spirit?
Answer: All believers.

2. What is the anointing of the Holy Spirit?
Answer: To consecrate (prepare) and sanctify (set apart) for service unto the Lord. A lot of Christians are not in service for the Lord but they have been set apart for service.

What is the Anointing

3. What is the filling of the Holy Spirit?
Answer: Indwelling empowerment.

4. When does the anointing of the Holy Spirit occur?
Answer: At the time of salvation.

In Whom ye also trusted, after that ye heard the word of truth, the Gospel of your salvation: in Whom also after that ye believed, ye were sealed with that holy Spirit of promise. (Ephesians 1:13)

Everything that the Holy Spirit provides is given when we receive salvation.

*And **ye are complete in Him**, which is the head of all principality and power.* (Colossians 2:10)

The Holy Spirit "*seals*" us because we are complete. He would not otherwise seal us.

Consider this: Have you ever needed a Notary Public?

If your document is incorrect or not complete, the notary will not seal it.

Where does the "***anointing***" occur?

"***Anointing***" for Christians takes place internally. It is the *internal designation* for service unto God. This means that the actual performance of service to God **is accomplished by the filling of the Holy Spirit**. We are "*filled*" with the Spirit through prayer and submissive yielding. We can and should be "*filled with the Spirit*" over and over again. The reason that we need to be constantly "*filled*" is because we are earthen vessels and we leak.

The "*filling of the Spirit*" is an important prayer for Christians. Most of the time we pray externally, "Lord, change this, or Lord fix that." Perhaps God may not want to change or fix anything. He may want to enable you from the inside to deal with the situation as it is.

Hence, in the common usage of the word "***anointing***," the meaning is most often a description of the *"filling of the Spirit."* As stated previously, we do not have the right to re-label theological themes or interchange Biblical definitions.

Anointing Equates to Selection

Our government once used the Selective Service Department to induct young men of a certain age into military service. **In order to be selected, a person had to be born an American citizen.**

How are we selected for service to the Lord?

We must be born again. We must be saved.

When we accept Christ, we are saved, selected and set aside. We are prepared by the various gifts the Holy Spirit whether we serve or not.

Unfortunately, some people are not serving, but this does not mean that the Holy Spirit has not *"anointed"* them. Every Christian has been *"anointed"* (designated) for service to the Lord. We all may not be serving, but we have all been selected for service.

The Baptism of the Holy Spirit Equates to Security

For by one Spirit are we all baptized into one body, whether we be Jews or Greeks, whether we be bond or free; and have been all made to drink into one Spirit. (1 Corinthians 12:13)

The baptism of the Holy Ghost is when a believer is placed into the Body of Christ (the Church). It's not rolling on the floor, standing on your head or speaking in *"unknown tongues."*

The baptism of the Holy Spirit is for our *security.*

An interesting and ironic observation is the people responsible for overemphasizing the ministry of the Holy Spirit are the ones who don't think they are secure by His ministry. They are usually the ones who think they can lose salvation and lose the *"anointing."*

Not so.

One of the *functions* of the Holy Spirit is *to secure us.* After all,

What is the Anointing

it is the Holy Spirit who "*seals us*" and is the "*earnest*" of **our inheritance until the day of redemption**.

The Filling of the Spirit Equates to Service

The "*filling of the Spirit*" enables us to live and labor for God. The "*filling of the Spirit*" provides *empowerment from within the believer*. We should continuously pray for the "*filling of the Spirit*." This should be at the top of our prayer list.

In the same sense that Paul defended his apostleship by stating he was not lacking anything that would diminish his authenticity as an apostle, we can declare with certainty, according to God's Word, that we are not lacking in anything regarding salvation or the ministry of the Holy Spirit. The essence of our assurance is the Word of God.

Perhaps one of the areas of uncertainty for Christians is the ministry of the Holy Spirit. We also have assurance that we have all that He provides and performs, including the baptism of the Holy Spirit and, especially, "*the anointing*."

You do not have to seek "*the anointing*." You do not have to stretch and strain to keep "*the anointing*."

The fact that you may be passing through some "troubled waters" on your pilgrimage doesn't mean that you are not "*anointed*."

The fact that you are experiencing a temporary set back financially doesn't mean that you are not "*anointed*."

Marital problems don't mean that you lost "*the anointing*."

The journey of a Christian is sometimes up and sometimes down. The Christian experience will not be without challenges, and hardships are not an indication that you don't have, or have lost, "*the anointing*."

You are simply experiencing life in this real world. Let your assurance come from the Word of God.

VII
The Sabbath Observance

There is scarcely a Christian who has not been challenged, or at least questioned, concerning the observance of the Sabbath. Some Christian groups actually observe the Sabbath; they worship on Saturday. However, the vast majority of Christians, obviously, do not observe the Sabbath. It is unfortunate that very little is taught regarding why it is not necessary to observe the Sabbath, especially in comparison to the amount of teaching supporting such observance.

The controversy dates back to the first century when Christianity was confronted with the matter of the proper, or correct, day of worship – and observances of Old Testament religious practices. Early Christians were, in particular, challenged about the rite of circumcision and worship on the Sabbath Day.

Since Christianity emerged out of Judaism – the first Christians being Jews – one of the first controversies had to do with admittance of Gentiles (anyone who is not Jewish) into the new faith. The centuries of old religious practices that the Jews were to maintain to ensure separation from Gentiles made it a volatile controversy. Those same religious practices turned into racial (ethnic) prejudices.

Some of the early Jewish Christians did not think that a Gentile could be saved. Later they softened their position concerning the salvation of Gentiles, but included the regulation that Gentiles would have to observe the old Jewish rite of circumcision to be saved. This caused Paul to pitch a holy fit.

And certain men which came down from Judea and taught the brethren, and said, "Except ye be circumcised after the manner of Moses, ye cannot be saved." When therefore Paul and Barnabas had no small dissension and disputation with them, they determined that Paul and Barnabas, and certain other of them, should go up to Jerusalem unto the apostles and elders about this question. But there rose up certain of the sect of the Pharisees, which believed, saying, That it was needful to circumcise them, and to command them to keep the law of Moses. (Acts 15:1,2,5)

Of course, included in the "Law of Moses" was the command to keep the Sabbath. However, salvation by grace alone prevailed, and the council of the apostles and elders ruled that it was not necessary for the Gentiles to keep the Law to be saved.

And they wrote letters by them after this manner; "The apostles and elders and brethren send greeting unto the brethren which are of the Gentiles in Antioch and Syria and Cilicia: Forasmuch as we have heard, that certain which went out from us have troubled you with words, subverting your souls, saying, 'Ye must be circumcised, and keep the law:' to whom we gave no such commandment."
(Acts 15:23,24)

The Sabbath Observance

Nevertheless, the controversy about keeping the Sabbath still endures among Christians today. In all fairness, it is a fact that most Christians who worship on the Lord's Day are not as reverent all through the day as they could and should be. Many Christians, after putting in an hour at Church, are done. A lot of us tune in to the football games on our car radios before we even leave the Church parking lot.

We could probably learn a lesson or two about reverence for the Lord's Day from Christians who do keep the Sabbath. Christians work, play, enjoy sports, and party rigorously on the Lord's Day. That needs to charge. We should be more reverent on this special day.

But, to help to understand the original meaning for keeping the Sabbath, we must understand that the meaning was progressive.

1) **It was designed by God as the day the work of creation ended**. (Genesis 2:2)

2) **It was distinguished by God as a uniquely blessed day.** (Genesis 2:3)

3) **It was developed by God to relate to freedom from Egyptian bondage.**

*"**And remember that thou wast a servant in the land of Egypt**, and that the Lord thy God brought thee out thence through a mighty hand and by a stretched out arm: therefore the Lord thy God commanded thee to keep the Sabbath Day."* (Deuteronomy 5:15)

No Christian could ever keep the Sabbath Day in remembrance of freedom from Egyptian bondage.

4) **It was dedicated by God to be a special day of rest.**

"Remember the Sabbath Day, to keep it holy. Six days shalt thou

*labour, and do all thy work: but the seventh day is the Sabbath of the Lord thy God: in it thou shalt not do any work, thou, nor thy son, nor thy daughter, thy manservant, nor thy maidservant, nor thy cattle, nor thy stranger that is within thy gates: **for in six days the Lord made the Heaven and Earth, the sea, and all that is in them is, and rested the seventh day**: wherefore the Lord blessed the Sabbath Day and hallowed it."* (Exodus 20:8-11)

5) It was demanded by God as a sign of his covenant with Israel.

*"**Moreover also I gave them my Sabbaths, to be a sign between Me and them**, that they might know that I am the Lord that sanctify them."* (Ezekiel 20:12)

*"Speak thou also unto the Children of Israel, saying, Verily My Sabbaths ye shall keep: **for it is a sign between Me and you throughout your generations**; that ye may know that I am the Lord that doth sanctify you."* (Exodus 31:13)

6) It is described as a "shadow of things to come."

*Let no man therefore judge you in meat, or in drink, or in respect of a holyday, or of the new moon, or of the Sabbath Days: **which are a shadow of things to come**; but the body is of Christ.* (Colossians 2:16,17)

7) It is the designation of salvation apart from works.

*There remaineth therefore a rest to the people of God. For he that is **entered** into his rest, he also hath **ceased from his own works**, as God did from His.* (Hebrews 4:9,10)

The Sabbath as a Memorial for Creation

The Sabbath Observance

Included in the creation story is the special significance that God placed on the seventh day. It later came to be known as the Sabbath Day. It is derived from the Hebrew word for "*rest*." It is the seventh day rest.

Genesis says that at the end of creation, God rested (Genesis 2:2). However, as the progressive meaning for the Sabbath developed in Scripture, we can see when the meaning of God's rest became an example for man.

Obviously, God does not need to rest.

Hast thou not known? Hast thou not heard, that the everlasting God, the Lord, the Creator of the ends of the earth, fainteth not, neither is weary? There is no searching of His understanding. (Isaiah 40:28)

The Psalmist says, "*He neither slumbers or sleeps.*"

We can conclude that when God rested at the end of creation, He did not rest because He was tired. God rested as a memorial of creation.

The Sabbaths that Moses Commanded

We must recognize that the Sabbaths that Moses commanded were given by revelation from God.

I recall speaking with a lady who believed in worshipping on the Sabbath Day. I asked her why she didn't keep any of the other laws that were commanded by Moses.

She attempted to make a distinction between Moses' Law (sometimes called The "Ceremonial Law"), and God's Law. She said that the 10 Commandments are God's Laws, but the Ceremonial Laws are for Israel. However, every law that Moses wrote was given to him by revelation of God. She was attempting to make a muted distinction between the two.

The critical fact to grasp about the Old Testaments laws is what they symbolically mean to Christians today. The fulfillment of all the laws was literally completed in Jesus Christ.

After the Genesis narrative, resting on the Sabbath Day is not mentioned again until Exodus 12. The Sabbaths (plural) that Moses commanded have fulfilled meaning in the complete work of Jesus Christ. Moses commanded seven Sabbaths to be observed other than the original seventh day Sabbath. These other Sabbaths are mentioned in Exodus and repeated again in Leviticus 23.

"And in the first day there shall be a holy convocation, and in the seventh day there shall be a holy convocation to you; no manner of work shall be done in them, except that which every man must eat, that only may be done of you." (Exodus 12:16)

These instructions are about additional Sabbaths that Israel was to observe by doing *"no manner of work."* Exodus 12:16 consists of commandments for the observance of the Feast of Unleavened Bread. This feast followed the Passover which occurred on the 15 day of *Nisan* and was to be observed as Sabbath day no matter what day of the week it came. Additionally, the Feast of Unleavened Bread, which was a seven-day feast, had two days that were to be observed as Sabbath days, the first day and the last day. Which means they were not to do any work on those days in the same way that they didn't work on the Passover or the Seventh Day Sabbath.

In addition to the Sabbath that Moses commanded that was included in the 10 Commandments in Exodus 20:8-11, the fourth Commandment. The 10 Commandments were not given until the Israelites reached Mt. Sinai.

"Remember the Sabbath Day, to keep it holy. Six days shalt thou labour, and do all thy work: but the seventh day is the Sabbath of the Lord thy God; in it thou shalt not do any work, thou, nor thy son, nor thy daughter, thy manservant, nor thy maidservant, nor thy cattle, nor thy stranger that is within thy gates: for in six days the Lord made the Heaven and Earth, the sea, and all that is in them is, and rested the seventh day: wherefore the Lord blessed the Sabbath Day, and hallowed it." (Exodus 20:8-11)

Here you can see that the Sabbath Day rest is connected to God's "rest" after creation. God later commanded that the seventh day Sabbath be observed as a sign between them.

> *"Wherefore the children of Israel shall keep the Sabbath, to observe the Sabbath throughout their generations, for a perpetual covenant. It is a sign between Me and the children of Israel for ever: for in six days the Lord made Heaven and Earth, and on the seventh day He rested and was refreshed."* (Exodus 31:16-17)

The progressive meaning that developed for keeping the Sabbath went from the memorial of the story of creation to the message of the sign of the covenant.

Signs accompanied all of God's covenants with Israel.

The rainbow was the sign for the covenant with Noah (Noahic).

Circumcision was the sign for the covenant with Abraham (Abrahamic).

The Sabbath was the sign for the covenant with Moses (Mosiac).

The virgin birth was the sign for the covenant with David (Davidic).

The Blood is the sign of the new covenant for Christians.

In addition to the Sabbaths that Moses commanded that was to be kept in observance with the Passover, there were two more Sabbaths to be kept in observance of the Feast of Unleavened Bread.

> *"These are the feasts of the Lord, even holy convocations, which ye shall proclaim in their seasons. In the fourteenth day of the first month at even is the Lord's Passover. And on the fifteenth day of the same month is the Feast of Unleavened Bread unto the Lord: seven days ye must eat unleavened bread. In the first day ye shall have a holy convocation: ye shall do no servile work therein. But ye shall offer an offering made by fire unto the Lord seven days. In the seventh day is a holy convocation: ye shall do no servile work therein."*

A Dose of Doctrine

(Leviticus 23:4-8)

Immediately following the Passover, the "Feast of Unleavened Bread" began and ended with a Sabbath observance. Needless to say, the fulfillments of the Sabbaths that began and ended the "Feast of Unleavened Bread" were complete in the work of Jesus Christ.

The Sabbath in Memory of Captivity

The progressive meaning of the Sabbath continues and includes the fact that Israel was to keep the Sabbath in memory of their captivity in Egypt. As they remembered their bondage, they were also to remember their deliverance by God.

Their deliverance from slavery illustrates salvation.

The apostle Paul briefly makes the connection between their deliverance from slavery in Egypt to our deliverance from sin. He says, *"Christ, our Passover is sacrificed for us, let us keep the feast."*

"And remember that thou wast a servant in the and Egypt, and that the Lord thy God brought thee out thence through a mighty hand and by a stretched out arm: Therefore the Lord thy God commanded thee to keep the Sabbath Day." (Deuteronomy 5:15)

God delivered them from labor to rest. The rest that they would enjoy as free people in Canaan replaced the labor they performed while slaves in Egypt. That does not mean that they did not work in Canaan – they did work. In fact, they had a very commendable work ethic. *The difference, however, is that they worked as free people. They did not work to become free.*

The simple purpose for the command of Moses in Deuteronomy was so they would not forget their deliverance. So we will not forget our deliverance, Jesus said, regarding the Lord's Supper, *"This, do in remembrance of me."*

It is unreasonable for Christians to think that they can keep the Sabbath for the purposes that Moses gave to Israel. This is underscored in the fact that the Scriptures show a progressive develop-

142

The Sabbath Observance

ment in meaning for the Sabbath observance. The Sabbath observance was for a memorial regarding the story of creation – and it was a message of the sign of the covenant in memory of slavery in Egypt.

The Sabbath Meaning for Christians

The Lord's teaching on the Sabbath changed the meaning for Christians. It is summarized in Mark 2:27.

And He said to them, "The Sabbath was made for man, and not man for the Sabbath."

In the days of Jesus, numerous restrictions had been added to the commandments of Moses to keep the Sabbath. Therefore, Jesus explained that the Sabbath was made for man, not man for the Sabbath. He said:

"Therefore the Son of Man is Lord also of the Sabbath." (Mark 2:28)

One of the main evidences of the Lord's sovereignty is what He chooses to change. There isn't anything that He is not Lord over, including the Sabbath.

For example, the Lord's death changed the entire meaning of the temple. The temple was at the center of Jewish life, but the Lord's death changed the purpose and the function for the temple.

But this man, after He had offered one sacrifice for sins forever, sat down on the right hand of God. (Hebrews 10:12)

No priest ever sat down in the Holy of Holies after making an animal sacrifice. Jesus changed the meaning of the Old Testament sacrificial system. There is no longer any need for temple worship or the sacrificial system that took place in the temple.

The Lord also changed the entire meaning and purpose of the Passover:

And as they were eating, Jesus took bread, and blessed it, and brake it, and gave it to the disciples, and said, "Take, eat; this is my body." And He took the cup, and gave thanks, and gave it to them saying, "Drink ye all of it; for this is my blood of the New Testament (covenant) which is shed for many for the remission of sins."
(Matthew 26:26-28)

The Scripture says, "*As they were eating.*"

As they were eating what?

The answer: the Passover meal, of course.

While they were eating the Passover, Jesus changed the meaning of the event. Jesus took bread and broke it and said, "*This is my body.*" He then took the cup and said, "*This is my blood.*"

When He spoke those words it was no longer the Old Testament Passover; He changed the meaning. The Passover that Moses commanded Israel to keep throughout their generations was changed from its symbolical meaning to the literal. Jesus is literally our Passover. (1 Corinthians 5:8).

Through His vicarious death, Jesus completely changed all of the Old Testament meanings of the Sabbath.

A point that is usually made by Christians who worship on the Sabbath is that Jesus kept the Sabbath.

And he came to Nazareth, where he had been brought up: and, as His custom was, He went into the synagogue on Sabbath Day, as His custom was, and stood up for to read. (Luke 4:16)

This is a favorite verse for proof that Jesus kept the Sabbath, and to that we say, "Of course He did." Jesus lived in complete submission to the Law. More important is the fact that Jesus completely fulfilled the Law. *Ceremonially* and *symbolically*, Jesus was the *literal fulfillment* of the Law. The Law was the shadow, but the Lord is the substance.

The Sabbath Observance

But when the fullness of the time was come, God sent forth His Son,
made of a woman, made under the law, to redeem them that were
under the law, that we might receive the adoption of sons.
(Galatians 4:4-5)

Christians who worship on the Sabbath also say that the apostle Paul kept the Sabbath. The Book of Acts plainly shows that when Paul arrived at a new location, he went to the synagogue on the Sabbath Day.

His main purpose for going to the synagogue, however, was to reach the Jews with the Gospel of Jesus Christ. The Jews who were in the synagogue were not engaging in Christian worship. They were still performing the Old Testament Jewish rituals. They were still burning incense, ringing bells and blowing the rams horn and offering sacrifices that can never take away sins.

Paul certainly didn't go into the synagogue to blow a rams horn, burn incense or to ring bells. And, most certainly, he absolutely did not go to sacrifice an animal. If he had gone to the synagogue for Jewish worship, he would not have been nearly beaten to death more times than we can count. His purpose for going into the synagogue on the Sabbath was to preach to Jews.

At the point of their final rejection of the Gospel, Paul said:

"Henceforth, I will go unto the Gentiles." (Acts 18:6)

Once his ministry of the Jews was ended, there was no need for him to go into the synagogue any longer.

What right do we have to change the worship day from the Sabbath to Sunday?

This question is often asked by Christians who worship of the Sabbath. However, there was never a change of worship days for the Gentiles. The change was for the Jews. And, Leviticus 23 holds the clue to the change.

"And he shall wave the sheaf before the Lord, to be accepted for you: on

the morrow after the Sabbath the priest shall wave it." (Leviticus 23:11)

In addition to the Passover and the "Feast of Unleavened Bread," Moses also introduced the "Feast of First Fruits." This feast was to begin the next day after the Sabbath (the seventh day Sabbath). According to modern calendars, the equivalent to that day is Sunday. However, the time element for Moses' instructions was long before there was a solar or lunar calendar.

It was many centuries before pagans worshipped the sun. This is said to be the origin of "SUN-DAY."

From its inception, the "Feast of First Fruits" always began the day after the Sabbath. It is not true to say that the early Church councils got together and "changed the day."

Furthermore, all of the Gospel accounts show that the Lord rose on the first day of the week. That was the day after the Sabbath, and the first day of the celebration of the "Feast of First Fruits." The apostle Paul supplies the Christian theology for waving the sheaf on the next day after the Sabbath. This was the first day of celebration for the "Feast of First Fruits."

But now is Christ risen from the dead, and become the firstfruits of them that slept. (1 Corinthian 15:20)

The "Feast of First Fruits" pointed to the day that Jesus would rise from the dead. Therefore, Christ is the "first fruits" of them that slept, meaning Christ is the first to be resurrected from the dead.

Granted, there are occasions (miracles) in the Old Testament and New Testament of people who came back to life. We sometimes mistakenly call these instances "resurrections," but they were merely restorations. Those people were merely restored to life – and **they all died again and are still dead**.

The only person who has been resurrected from the dead is Jesus Christ.

Authentic resurrection includes having a glorified body. All the other people who were restored to life came back in their original corrupted bodies.

The Sabbath Observance

The first appearances of the resurrected Lord to His disciples occurred on *the first day of the week.*

Then, the same day at evening, being the first day of the week, when the doors were shut where the disciples were assembled for fear of the Jews, came Jesus and stood in the midst, and saith unto them, "Peace be unto you." (John 20:19)

There is another feast from the list in Leviticus 23 (actually there are seven) that relates to the first day of the week. It is Pentecost.

"And ye shall count unto you from the morrow after the Sabbath, from the day that ye brought the sheaf of the wave offering; seven Sabbaths shall be complete: even unto the morrow after the seventh Sabbath shall ye number fifty days; and ye shall offer a new meat offering unto the Lord." (Leviticus 23:15,16)

This was the "Feast of Weeks," commonly known as Pentecost. The instruction for counting is to start with the next day after the Sabbath, up to the day after the seventh Sabbath – seven full weeks.

Pentecost – like the "Feast of First Fruits" – also began the next day after the seventh Sabbath, making it the first day of the week. Of course, most Christians are more familiar with Pentecost from Acts 2 than from Leviticus 23.

The Church (Christian Dispensation) came into being on Pentecost. Pentecost is commonly called "the birthday of the Church."

And when the Day of Pentecost was fully come, they were all with one accord in one place. And suddenly there came a sound from Heaven as of a rushing mighty wind, and it (the wind) filled all the house where they were sitting. And there appeared unto them cloven tongues like as of fire, and it (symbolic fire) sat upon each of them. And they were all filled with the Holy Ghost, and began to speak with other (not

147

unknown) *tongues, as the Spirit gave them utterance.* (Acts 2:1-4)

The disciples (about 120) were baptized into the spiritual organism of the Church on the Day of Pentecost.

It is difficult to accurately determine how many years had past between Acts 2 to Acts 20. It is clear, however, that at this time the disciples had already begun to worship on the first day of the week.

And upon the first day of the week, when the disciples came together to break bread, Paul preached unto them, ready to depart on the morrow; and continued his speech until midnight. (Acts 20:7)

The context of Acts 20 shows that Paul was in Troas for seven days. But, neither he nor the local Christians apparently met for the breaking of bread until the first day of the week.

And we sailed away from Philippi after the days of unleavened bread, and came unto them to Troas in five days; where we abode seven days. (Acts 20:6)

It is equally difficult to accurately determine how many years had passed between Acts 2 to the events in 1 Corinthians 16. However, the indication is that the Corinthian Christians were also worshipping on the first day of the week.

Upon the first day of the week let every one of you lay by him in store, as God has prospered him, that there be no gatherings when I come. (1 Corinthians 16:2)

The Sabbath Day symbolizes and definitely illustrates salvation apart from works. This is what makes up our Christian heritage. The Epistle to the Hebrews was predominantly written for Jewish Christians who were being persuaded by the Judaizers to return to the Law. It is a letter full of urgings to remain steadfast in their new faith in Jesus Christ.

The Sabbath Observance

"But Christ as Son over His own house; whose house are we, if we hold fast to the confidence and the rejoicing of the hope firm unto the end. (Hebrews 3:6)

For we are made partakers of Christ if we hold the beginning of our confidence stedfast unto the end. (Hebrews 3:14)

Cast not away therefore your confidence, which hath great recompence of reward. (Hebrews 10:35)

The message to the Hebrew Christians was that they were on the right track. They had made the right decision to accept Jesus Christ. Their faith was focused in the right direction; they simply needed to "hold on."

Hebrews 3 and 4 deal extensively with the Christian meaning of the Sabbath Day. The writer goes into exhaustive detail to show that the Sabbath Day is only an illustration of salvation through faith in Jesus Christ. The following verses are a direct reference to Psalm 95:7-10.

And to whom sware He that they should not enter into His rest, but to them that believed not? So we see that they could not enter in because of unbelief. (Hebrews 3:18,19)

The main emphasis of chapters 3 and 4 is the complete spiritual (Christian) meaning of "rest."

Who did God swear would not enter into his rest?
Israel.
Why did God not allow them to enter into His rest?
It was because of their unbelief.

These verses show that belief was the essential element that was required for them to enter Canaan and that belief is the essential element to enter into the rest symbolized by the Sabbath.

The writer digs even deeper into the real meaning of the Sabbath.

For unto us (Jews in New Testament times) *was the Gospel preached, as well as unto them* (Jews in Old Testament times)*: but the word preached did not profit them, not being mixed with faith in them that heard it. For we which have believed do enter rest, as He said, "As I have sworn in my wrath, if they shall enter into My rest: although the works were finished from the foundation of the world."*
(Hebrews 4:2-3)

Here again, the emphasis is upon faith. Faith is the essential element to enter in the rest that was foreshadowed by the Sabbath Day rest. The present tense reality of the Sabbath rest is in the words, *"For we who have believed do enter rest."* In other words, believers in Christ have already entered into the rest of salvation. We already have the rest that the Sabbath pointed to.

On the other hand, the opposite was not true for them who heard the word but did not mix it with faith. Verse 3 ends with what I will call an "extra dose of revelation." It is like when a winning team puts more "insurance points" on the scoreboard near the end of the game.

Although (I just want you to know) **the works were finished from the foundation of the world**.

That is not a reference to the six-day creation.
What works were finished from the foundation of the world?
The answer: the works of our salvation in Jesus Christ.
This fact is consistent with Revelation 13:8, which reads:

And all that dwell upon the earth shall worship him (Anti-Christ), *whose names are not written in the book of life of the Lamb slain from the foundation of the world.*

The meaning of Hebrews 4:8 is that the Sabbath Day rest of the

The Sabbath Observance

Old Testament, was not the essence, but rather, the example of our true rest in Jesus Christ.

For is Jesus (Joshua) had given them rest, then would he not afterward have spoken of another day.

If the rest Israel experienced in Canaan was the total meaning of rest that God had for them, He wouldn't have spoken of another day. Nevertheless, God had given Israel the promise of another day:

There remaineth therefore a rest to the people of God. (Hebrews 4:9)

There is an unequivocal "rest" beyond the rest of the Sabbath Day and the rest in Canaan. It is our rest in Jesus Christ for our salvation. It is the rest that He personally promised in His own words: "*Come unto me and I will give you rest.*"

The following verse clinches it:

*For he that is entered into his rest, he also **hath ceased from his own works, as God did from His**.* (Hebrews 4:10)

"Own works" for salvation cease when you have entered into His rest. We cease from our own works in the same sense that God ceased from His works after creation. God is our example of ceasing from works.

Resting on the Sabbath Day had a twofold purpose:

A. To rest from physical toil to **sustain** physical life.
B. To rest from physical toil to **secure** spiritual life.

While we *must toil for physical life, we cannot toil for spiritual life.* As well, we *must rest in faith* in the completed works that God has done for us to be saved. We can rest in the assurance that "*the works were finished from the foundation of the world.*"

*Let us labor therefore to enter into that rest, lest any man fall after the
same example of unbelief.* (Hebrews 4:11)

The point of this admonishment is, unfortunately, dulled by the
use of the word "*labor*." The theological flow from Hebrews 3:1 to
Hebrews 4:10 has been "*belief*" and "*rest*." It is rather diminishing
to suddenly be admonished to "*labor*" in order to enter into the rest
that God's works have provided.

The Greek word for "*labor*" that is used is "*spoudazo*." It appears
12 times in the New Testament, and this is the only time that it is
used to mean labor. Nine of the 12 times that it is used, it is translated to mean "*diligence*."

The context of these two chapters in Hebrews demands that it
should be translated to mean "*diligence*" here as well. "*Be diligent to
enter into God's rest and not fall after the example of unbelief.*"

This follows the flow of repeated urgings by the author of the
Book of Hebrews, to the Hebrew Christians to "hold on" and to be
"steadfast" in their confidence because the vital matter of entering
into rest (salvation) is either belief or unbelief.

The authorship of the epistle to the Hebrews has been an ongoing debate for several centuries. It has commonly been attributed to
the apostle Paul. If it was indeed written by Paul, he has the historical, cultural and theological background to wholeheartedly argue in
support of observing the Sabbath Day in the strictest traditions of
Jewish fervor. The record of his heritage shows that he was of the
stock of Israel, specifically of the tribe of Benjamin, circumcised on
the eighth day, a Hebrew of the Hebrews. He was of the most con-
servative form of Judaism, a Pharisee.

Paul was most certainly acquainted with the observance of the
Sabbath. As a former Pharisee, he would scarcely breathe on the
Sabbath Day. If anyone had the credentials to bear down on
Christians to keep the Sabbath Day, he was definitely that person.

However, none of Paul's epistles contain the slightest resem-
blance of admonishments, urgings or warnings for Christians to
keep the Sabbath Day. To the Colossian Christians he wrote:

The Sabbath Observance

Beware lest any man spoil you through philosophy and vain deceit, after the tradition of men, after the rudiments of the world, and not after Christ. For in Him dwelleth all the fullness of the Godhead bodily. And ye are complete in Him, which is the head of all principality and power. (Colossians 2:8-10)

Paul's warning was for Christians to "beware" of being "spoiled" through teaching that is not according to Christ. "Beware" is an urgent warning. "Beware" means to watch out, to be on your guard.

In other words, **beware** if someone is "on your case" about worshiping on the wrong day.

Beware if someone is trying to persuade you that you must speak in so-called "***tongues***" to be saved.

Beware if someone attempts to convince you that your salvation is not valid because you were baptized by the wrong formula.

Beware and be firm.

Paul writes, "*...you are complete in Him.*"

Complete means nothing needs to be added.

He further wrote:

*And you, being dead in your sins and the uncircumcision of your flesh, hath He quickened together with Him, having forgiven you all trespasses; blotting out the handwriting of ordinances that was against us, which was contrary to us, and took it out of the way, nailing it to His cross; and having spoiled principalities and powers, He made a shew of them openly, triumphing over them in it. **Let no man therefore judge you in meat, or in drink, or in respect of a holyday, or of the new moon, or of a Sabbath Days**: which are a shadow of things to come; but the body* (substance) *is of Christ.*
(Colossians 2:13-17)

The amazing thing is that a former Pharisee wrote those words. Because we have been made alive with Christ and have been forgiven of all trespasses, we should not allow anyone to judge us about anything – including the Sabbath Day. After all, the Sabbath Day, or Sabbath Days were, "*A shadow* (type or illustration) *of things to come.*"

Some years ago, when our daughter was a little girl, my parents flew in from San Antonio. This was the first time that they were to see their newest grandchild. While waiting for them in the airport terminal, we watched the airplane land. Pointing to the airplane, we said to our daughter, "Here they come."

As the door of the plane opened, we saw my father and mother walk down the steps. We pointed again and said, "Here they come."

As they made their way toward us in the corridor, we said, "Here they come."

However, when they finally reached us we started hugging and kissing and greeting each other because they who had been coming, had arrived.

This is the meaning of the Sabbath Day. Originally, the observance was for the *Creation*, then it turned to the *Convocations*, then to the *Captivity* and, finally, we have the *Completion*.

The Emancipation Proclamation signed by President Lincoln declares: "*All slaves are free.*"

The distressing reality was that many of the former slaves did not leave the plantations. They chose to remain in bondage (the truth is, some were not permitted to leave). Many Christians are like those former slaves in that they voluntarily stay in bondage.

The true meaning of the Sabbath Day rest is that we have entered into His rest. Yet, many Christians remain in bondage to the Sabbath Day observance as freed slaves chose to remain in bondage to a cruel slavery system.